The strongest bride on earth.
Sumomomo Momomo.1
Shinobu Ohtaka

CONTENTS

SUMOMOMO, MOMOMO

AS I FEARED...

PAKAAA ノ∧

I CAN ONLY SPLIT THE WATERFALL HALFWAY!!

ZAZAZAZAZAZAZAZA

ピタッ!
PITA (STOP)

PAKAAA GWISHHO

HUH!?

ACK!

NO!

IT'S BECAUSE YOU ARE A WOMAN, MOMOKO!

YOU CANNOT MASTER THE ARTS OF OUR CLAN!!

BI (ZIP)

HOWEVER, THERE IS ONE WAY TO AVOID THIS GRIM FATE!

NO!!

THIS CANNOT BE, FATHER!

AT THIS RATE, THE BLOOD AND SKILLS OF THE KUZU-RYUU LINE...

...ARE FATED TO GROW WEAKER AND WEAKER UNTIL THEY DIE OUT!

SFX: ZAZAZAZAZAZA

YOU MUST WED THE WORLD'S STRONGEST MAN AND BEAR THE WORLD'S STRONGEST HEIRS!!!

0. THE STRONGEST FIANCÉE ON EARTH

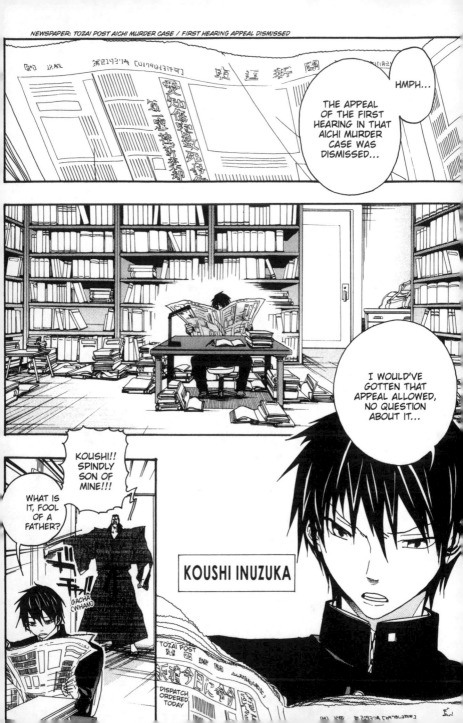

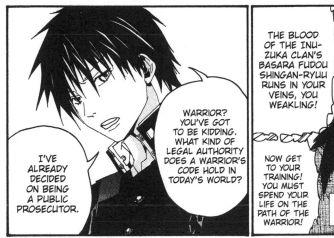

I'VE ALREADY DECIDED ON BEING A PUBLIC PROSECUTOR.

WARRIOR? YOU'VE GOT TO BE KIDDING. WHAT KIND OF LEGAL AUTHORITY DOES A WARRIOR'S CODE HOLD IN TODAY'S WORLD?

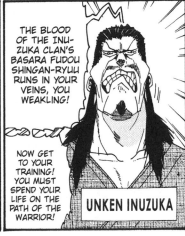

THE BLOOD OF THE INU-ZUKA CLAN'S BASARA FUDOU SHINGAN-RYUU RUNS IN YOUR VEINS, YOU WEAKLING!

NOW GET TO YOUR TRAINING! YOU MUST SPEND YOUR LIFE ON THE PATH OF THE WARRIOR!

UNKEN INUZUKA

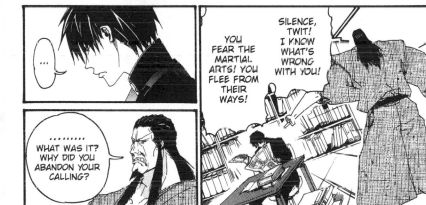

...

YOU FEAR THE MARTIAL ARTS! YOU FLEE FROM THEIR WAYS!

SILENCE, TWIT! I KNOW WHAT'S WRONG WITH YOU!

....

WHAT WAS IT? WHY DID YOU ABANDON YOUR CALLING?

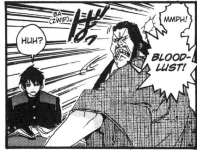

BA (ZWIP)—

HUH?

MMPH!

BLOOD-LUST!

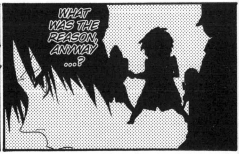

WHAT WAS THE REASON, ANYWAY...?

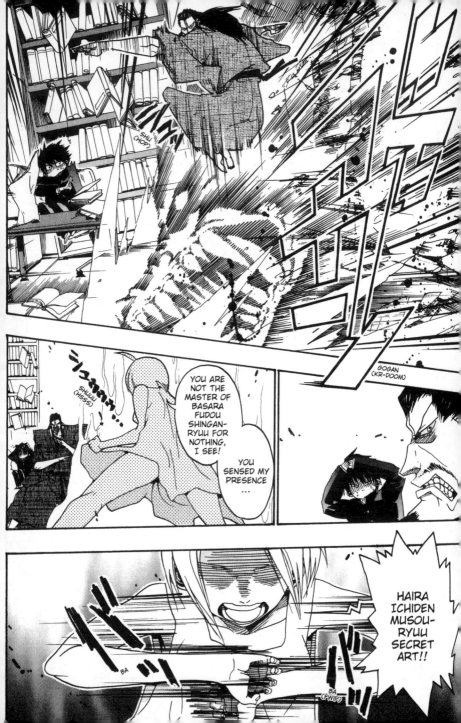

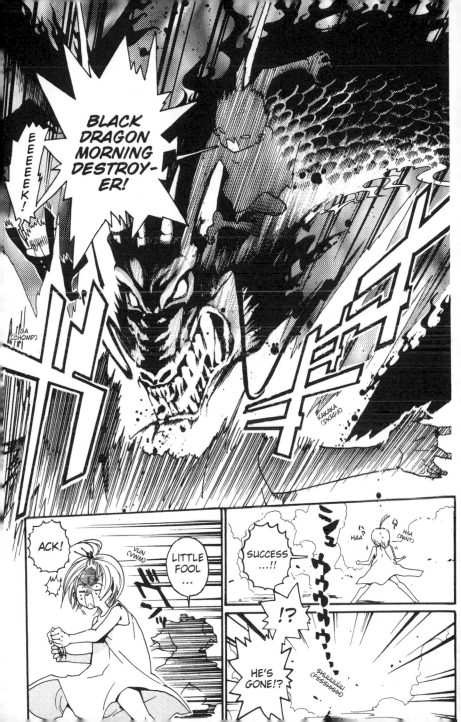

FORGIVE ME FOR EXHIBITING SUCH INFERIOR WORK! I HAVE MUCH TO LEARN...

I AM MOVED... BY YOUR SKILL!

GAKU (SLUMP)

URGH...

GYACK!

ブル ブル

じいん...!

T-THANK YOU...!

JIIN (TOUCHED)

DO NOT BELITTLE YOURSELF! YOUR SKILL IS IMPRESSIVE...

ドシャ

DOSHA (THWOMP)

I HAVE NO IDEA WHAT TO SAY...

YES, SIR! I AM LATE TO INTRODUCE MYSELF!

スク

SUKU (STAMP)

HAIRA STYLE, YOU SAID...? MIGHT YOU BE...

HUH?

I AM THE ONLY CHILD OF HAIRA ICHIDEN MUSOU-RYUU HEAD SENDAYUU KUZURYUU— MOMOKO KUZURYUU!!

BIKUUU (SHOCK)

HUHH-HHHH!!??

VERY WELL!!

YES! YES! YES!

OSU!!

I MUST EXPLAIN!

IT ALL HAPPENED AROUND THE TIME YOU WERE BORN...

W-WHAT THE HELL IS GOING ON HERE...?

I HAVE COME TO MAKE A CHILD WITH KOUSHI INUZUKA-DONO!!!

MOMOKO KUZURYUU

SFX: GUGUGUGUGUGU (SQUEEEEEZE)

H-HOW COULD YOU...!!?

I BELIEVE YOUR SON WOULD BE SUITABLE FOR MY DAUGHTER!!

I WAS THINKING THE SAME THING!!

GASHI (CLENCH)

BETROTHAL

I MADE A PACT WITH ANOTHER MAN...

SAME GOES FOR YOU!

N-NOT BAD!!

ZE (WHEEZE)

HAA (PANT)

ZE

W- WHY!?

GOTTA PACK FOR SCHOOL.

...UNLIKE YOU PEOPLE...

BECAUSE I HAVE A FULLY FUNCTIONAL, RATIONAL INTELLECT...

BOOK: MATH II

WHAAAAAAT!?

HAN (CHAK!)

ビクーン BIKUUUU (FLINCH)

HIKUU (TWITCH)

HMPH! I REFUSE.

バタン BATAN (SLAM)

LISTEN, DAD. I'M NOT DOING ANY MARTIAL ARTS.

AND I'M DEFINITELY NOT MARRYING THAT GIRL!!

KOUSHI, STRONG?

YOU OVER-ESTI-MATE HIM, GIRL.

MY WEAKNESS IS ILL-SUITED FOR KOUSHI-DONO'S GREAT STRENGTH...

GAKUUUU (SLUMP)

SOB SOB SOB

NO... KOUSHI-DONO...!

NO!

IT CANNOT BE! NOT KOUSHI-DONO!

IT IS A SAD SIGHT...

WHEN HE WITNESSES VIOLENCE, HIS LEGS TURN TO JELLY AND HE COWERS IN FEAR...

ALAS, IT IS TRUE.

HE IS WEAK! BOTH IN BODY AND SPIRIT...

HE MAY HAVE A SHARP TONGUE AND THE BRAINS TO USE IT, BUT THE CORE BENEATH IS ROTTEN...

KOUSHI-DONO-OOO!

BUT WHY!?

ROAD: STOP

SFX: TE (TMP) TE TE

KOUSHI-DONO HAS GIVEN UP ON THE MARTIAL ARTS!?

!?

HE HAS BEEN THUS EVER SINCE HE ABANDONED THE WAY OF THE WARRIOR...

YOU'RE CRAZY! WHY WOULD YOU WANT TO MARRY A GUY YOU JUST MET MINUTES AGO!?

GEEZ! GET OFF OF ME!!

HUH?

KOUSHI-DONO! KOUSHI-DONO! KOUSHI-DONO! KOUSHI-DONO! KOUSHI-DONO!

SFX: SHI (SHOO) SHI SHI

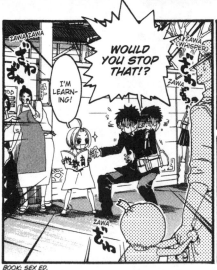

ZAWA ZAWA

WOULD YOU STOP THAT!?

ZAWA WHISPER

I'M LEARN-ING!

ZAWA

ZAWA

BOOK: SEX ED.

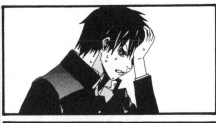

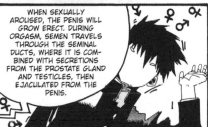

WHEN SEXUALLY AROUSED, THE PENIS WILL GROW ERECT. DURING ORGASM, SEMEN TRAVELS THROUGH THE SEMINAL DUCTS, WHERE IT IS COMBINED WITH SECRETIONS FROM THE PROSTATE GLAND AND TESTICLES, THEN EJACULATED FROM THE PENIS.

SFX: BUTSU (MUTTER) BUTSU

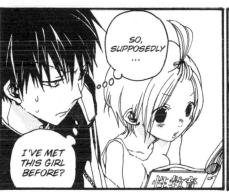

SO, SUPPOSEDLY ...

I'VE MET THIS GIRL BEFORE?

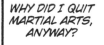

......
......

WHY DID I QUIT MARTIAL ARTS, ANYWAY?

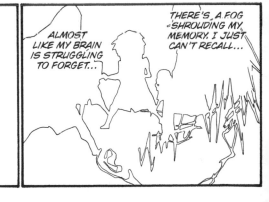

ALMOST LIKE MY BRAIN IS STRUGGLING TO FORGET...

THERE'S A FOG SHROUDING MY MEMORY. I JUST CAN'T RECALL...

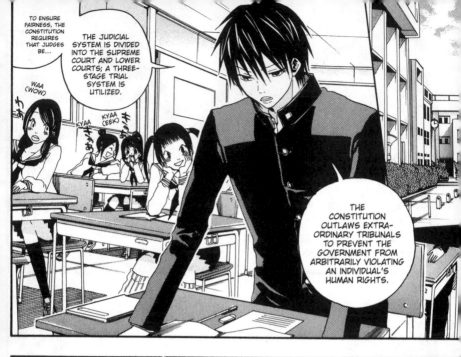

TO ENSURE FAIRNESS, THE CONSTITUTION REQUIRES THAT JUDGES BE...

THE JUDICIAL SYSTEM IS DIVIDED INTO THE SUPREME COURT AND LOWER COURTS; A THREE-STAGE TRIAL SYSTEM IS UTILIZED.

WAA (WOW)

KYAA (EEK)

THE CONSTITUTION OUTLAWS EXTRA-ORDINARY TRIBUNALS TO PREVENT THE GOVERNMENT FROM ARBITRARILY VIOLATING AN INDIVIDUAL'S HUMAN RIGHTS.

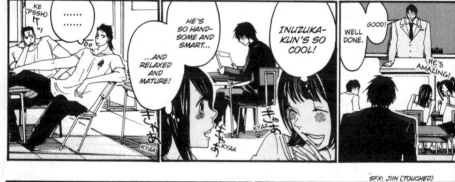

KE (PSSHD)

......

......

...AND RELAXED AND MATURE!

HE'S SO HAND-SOME AND SMART...

INUZUKA-KUN'S SO COOL!

KYAA

WELL DONE.

GOOD!

HE'S AMAZING!

SFX: JIIN (TOUCHED)

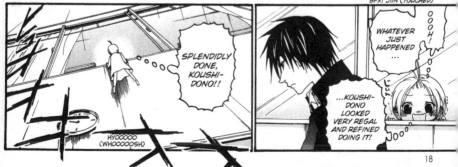

SPLENDIDLY DONE, KOUSHI-DONO!!

HYOOOOO (WHOOOOOSH)

WHATEVER JUST HAPPENED...

OOOH!

...KOUSHI-DONO LOOKED VERY REGAL AND REFINED DOING IT!

18

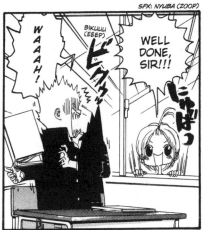

WAAAH!

BIKUUU (EEEP)

WELL DONE, SIR!!!

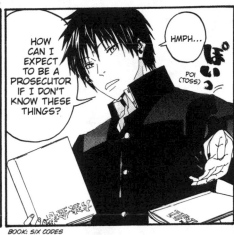

HOW CAN I EXPECT TO BE A PROSECUTOR IF I DON'T KNOW THESE THINGS?

HMPH...

POI (TOSS)

BOOK: SIX CODES

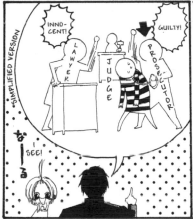

*SIMPLIFIED VERSION

INNO-CENT!

GUILTY!

LAWYER

JUDGE

PROSECUTOR

I SEE!

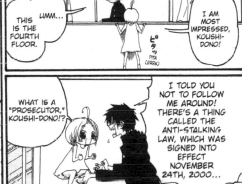

THIS IS THE FOURTH FLOOR.

UMM...

PITA (ORRK)

I AM MOST IMPRESSED, KOUSHI-DONO!

WHAT IS A "PROSECUTOR," KOUSHI-DONO!?

I TOLD YOU NOT TO FOLLOW ME AROUND! THERE'S A THING CALLED THE ANTI-STALKING LAW, WHICH WAS SIGNED INTO EFFECT NOVEMBER 24TH, 2000...

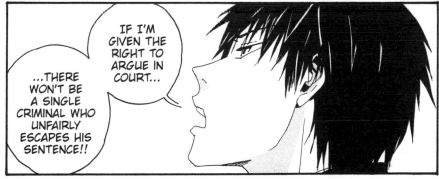

IF I'M GIVEN THE RIGHT TO ARGUE IN COURT...

...THERE WON'T BE A SINGLE CRIMINAL WHO UNFAIRLY ESCAPES HIS SENTENCE!!

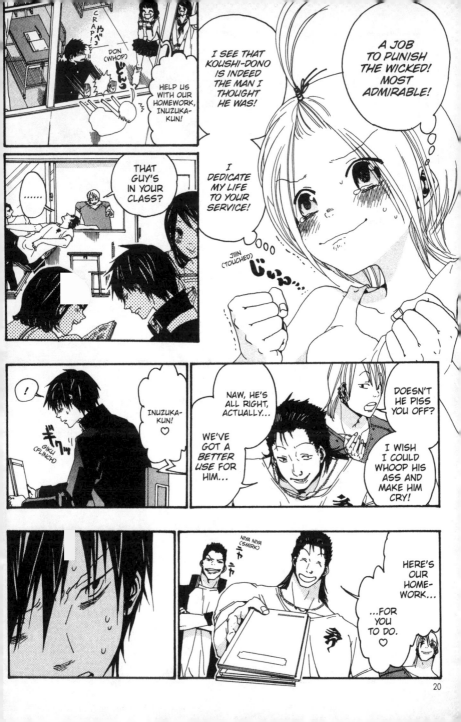

20

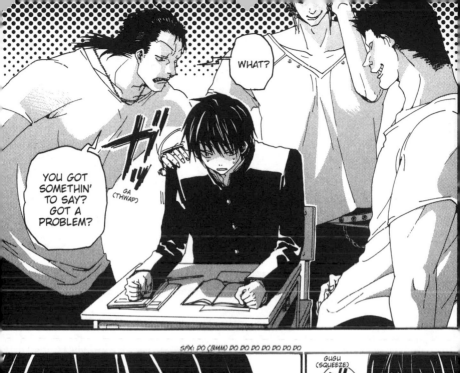

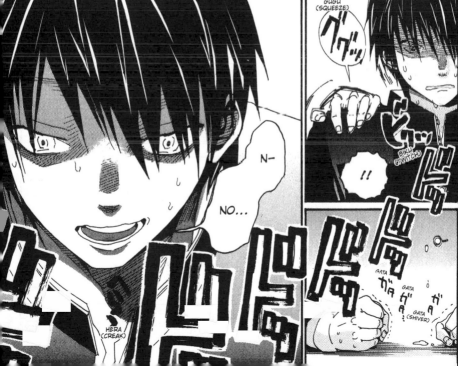

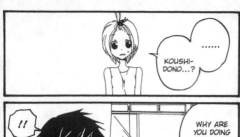

KOUSHI-DONO...?

......

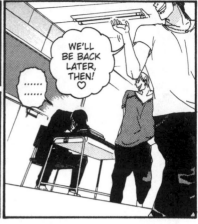

WE'LL BE BACK LATER, THEN! ♡

......

!!

WHY ARE YOU DOING THE HOMEWORK OF OTHERS?

GIKU (FLINCH)

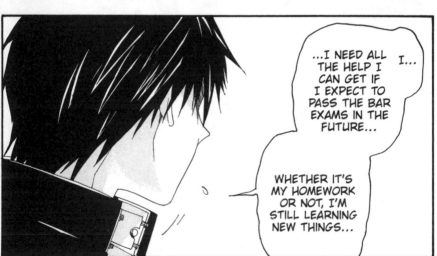

...I NEED ALL THE HELP I CAN GET IF I EXPECT TO PASS THE BAR EXAMS IN THE FUTURE...

I...

WHETHER IT'S MY HOMEWORK OR NOT, I'M STILL LEARNING NEW THINGS...

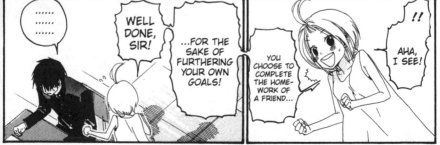

......
......
......

WELL DONE, SIR!

...FOR THE SAKE OF FURTHERING YOUR OWN GOALS!

YOU CHOOSE TO COMPLETE THE HOMEWORK OF A FRIEND...

!!

AHA, I SEE!

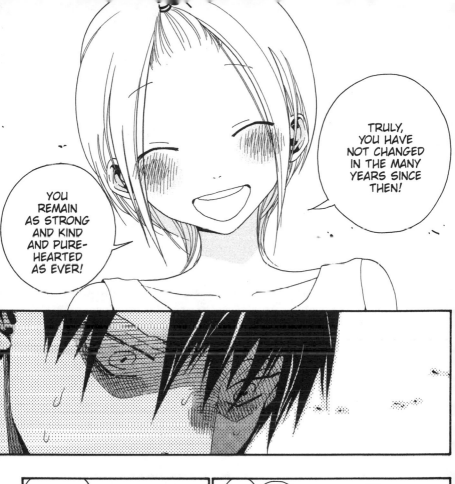

TRULY, YOU HAVE NOT CHANGED IN THE MANY YEARS SINCE THEN!

YOU REMAIN AS STRONG AND KIND AND PURE-HEARTED AS EVER!

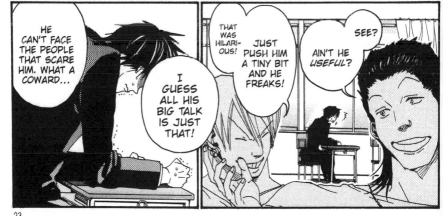

HE CAN'T FACE THE PEOPLE THAT SCARE HIM. WHAT A COWARD...

I GUESS ALL HIS BIG TALK IS JUST THAT!

THAT WAS HILARI-OUS!

JUST PUSH HIM A TINY BIT AND HE FREAKS!

AIN'T HE *USEFUL*?

SEE?

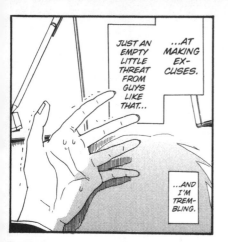

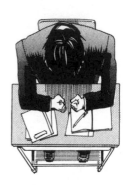

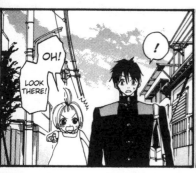

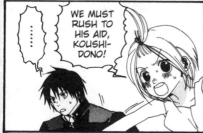

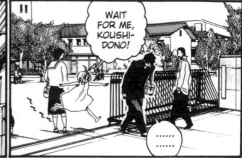

SFX: TE (TMP) TE TE TE

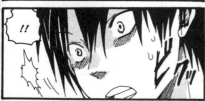

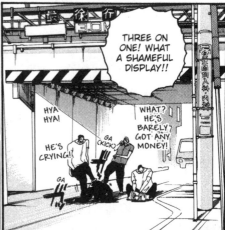

SFX: BIKU (SHIVER)

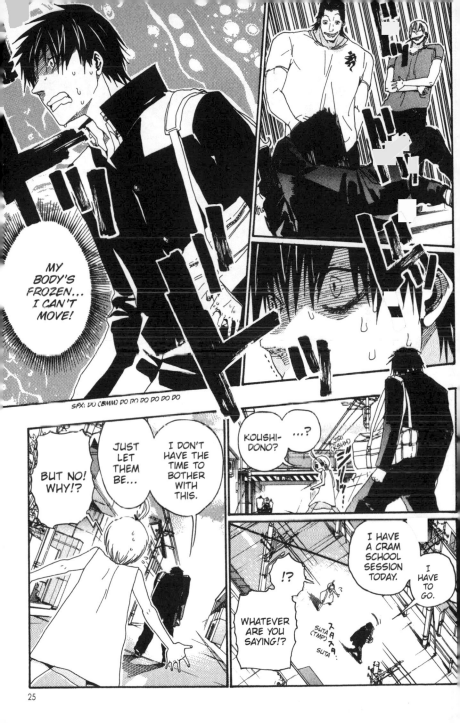

MY BODY'S FROZEN... I CAN'T MOVE!

SFX: DU (BMM) DO DO DO DO DO DO

BUT NO! WHY!?

JUST LET THEM BE...

I DON'T HAVE THE TIME TO BOTHER WITH THIS.

KOUSHI-DONO?

....?

I HAVE A CRAM SCHOOL SESSION TODAY.

I HAVE TO GO.

WHATEVER ARE YOU SAYING!?

!?

SUTA (TMP)

SUTA

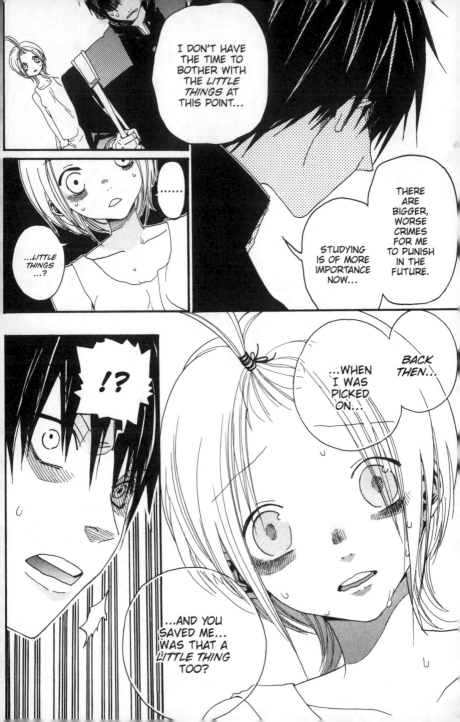

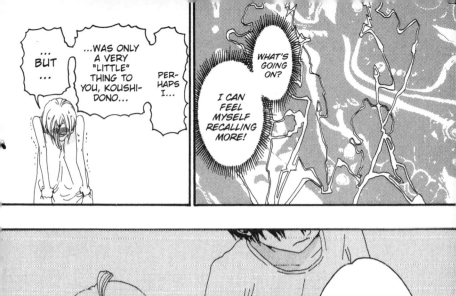

BUT...

...WAS ONLY A VERY "LITTLE" THING TO YOU, KOUSHI-DONO...

PER-HAPS I...

WHAT'S GOING ON?

I CAN FEEL MYSELF RECALLING MORE!

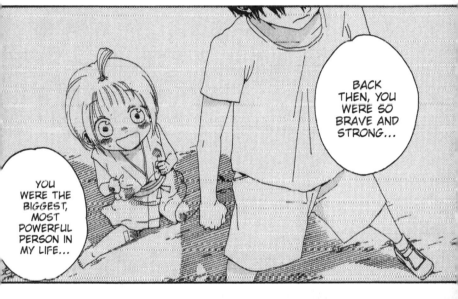

BACK THEN, YOU WERE SO BRAVE AND STRONG...

YOU WERE THE BIGGEST, MOST POWERFUL PERSON IN MY LIFE...

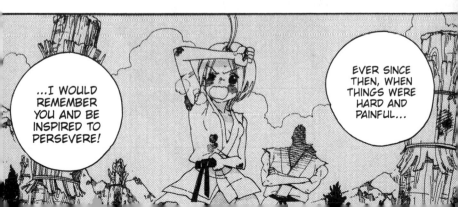

...I WOULD REMEMBER YOU AND BE INSPIRED TO PERSEVERE!

EVER SINCE THEN, WHEN THINGS WERE HARD AND PAINFUL...

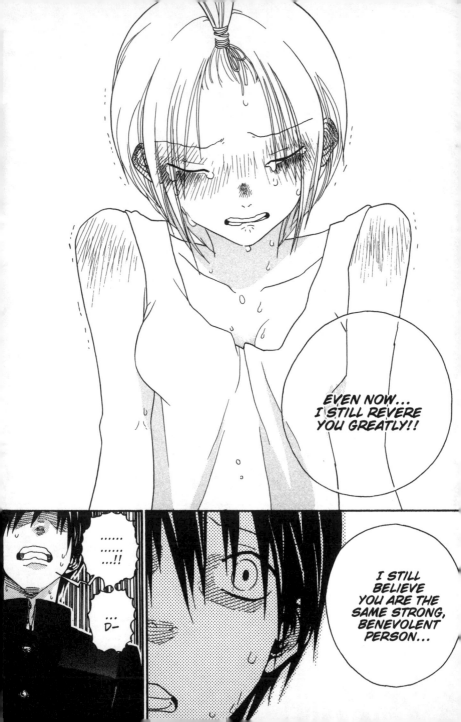

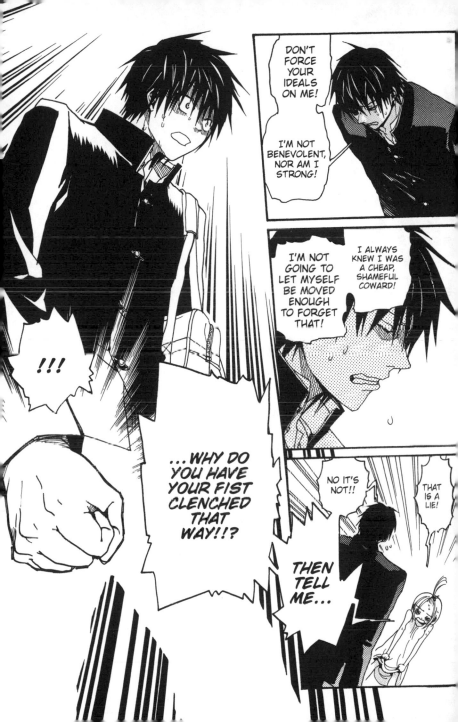

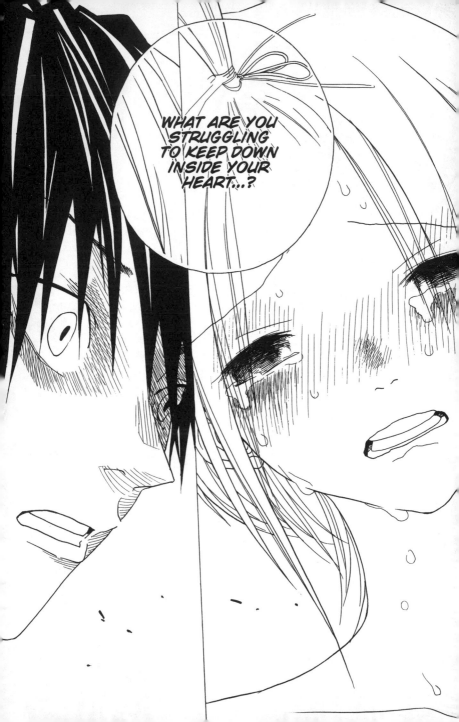

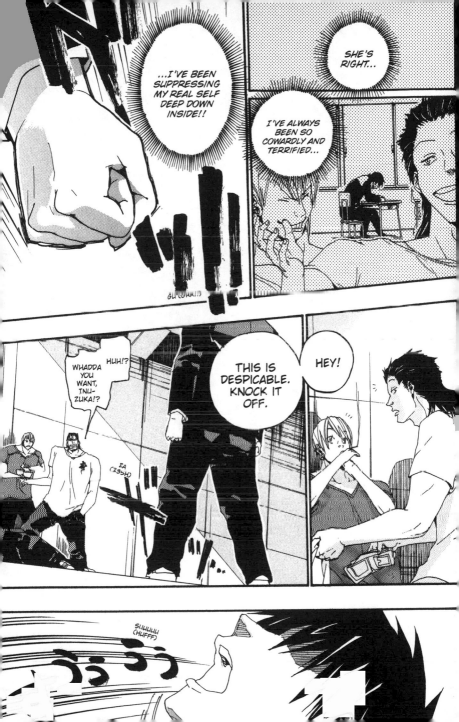

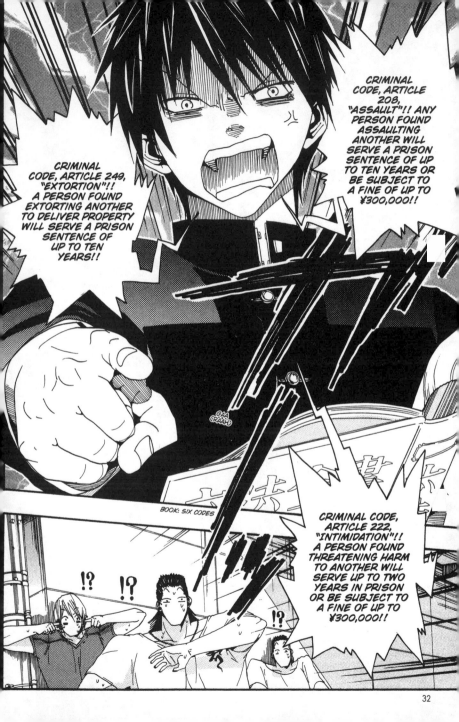

CRIMINAL CODE, ARTICLE 249, "EXTORTION"!! A PERSON FOUND EXTORTING ANOTHER TO DELIVER PROPERTY WILL SERVE A PRISON SENTENCE OF UP TO TEN YEARS!!

CRIMINAL CODE, ARTICLE 208, "ASSAULT"!! ANY PERSON FOUND ASSAULTING ANOTHER WILL SERVE A PRISON SENTENCE OF UP TO TEN YEARS OR BE SUBJECT TO A FINE OF UP TO ¥300,000!!

BOOK: SIX CODES

CRIMINAL CODE, ARTICLE 222, "INTIMIDATION"!! A PERSON FOUND THREATENING HARM TO ANOTHER WILL SERVE UP TO TWO YEARS IN PRISON OR BE SUBJECT TO A FINE OF UP TO ¥300,000!!

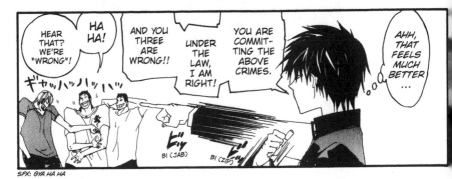

HEAR THAT? WE'RE "WRONG"!

HA HA!

AND YOU THREE ARE WRONG!!

UNDER THE LAW, I AM RIGHT!

YOU ARE COMMITTING THE ABOVE CRIMES.

AHH, THAT FEELS MUCH BETTER...

ギャッハッハッハッ

BI (JAB)

BI (ZIP)

SFX: GYA HA HA

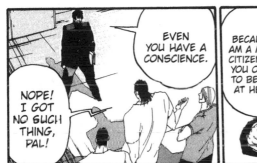
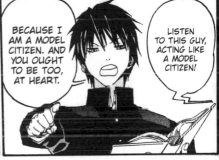

EVEN YOU HAVE A CONSCIENCE.

NOPE! I GOT NO SUCH THING, PAL!

BECAUSE I AM A MODEL CITIZEN. AND YOU OUGHT TO BE TOO, AT HEART.

LISTEN TO THIS GUY, ACTING LIKE A MODEL CITIZEN!

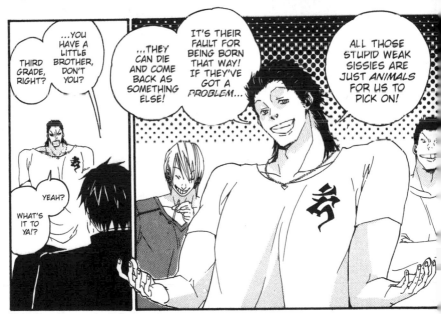

...YOU HAVE A LITTLE BROTHER, DON'T YOU?

THIRD GRADE, RIGHT?

...THEY CAN DIE AND COME BACK AS SOMETHING ELSE!

IT'S THEIR FAULT FOR BEING BORN THAT WAY! IF THEY'VE GOT A *PROBLEM*...

ALL THOSE STUPID WEAK SISSIES ARE JUST *ANIMALS* FOR US TO PICK ON!

YEAH?

WHAT'S IT TO YA!?

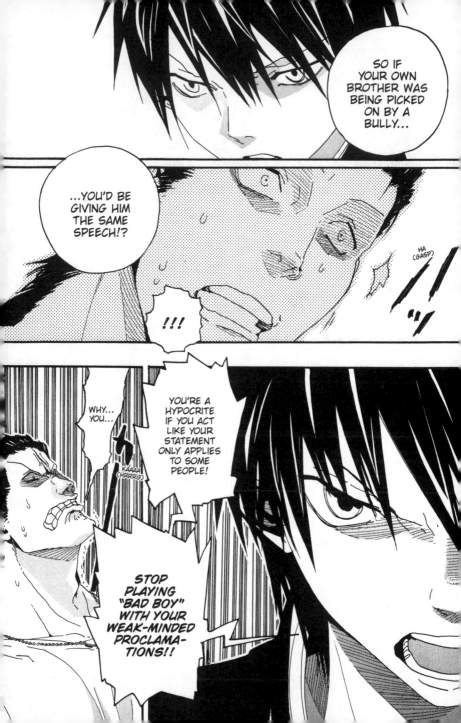

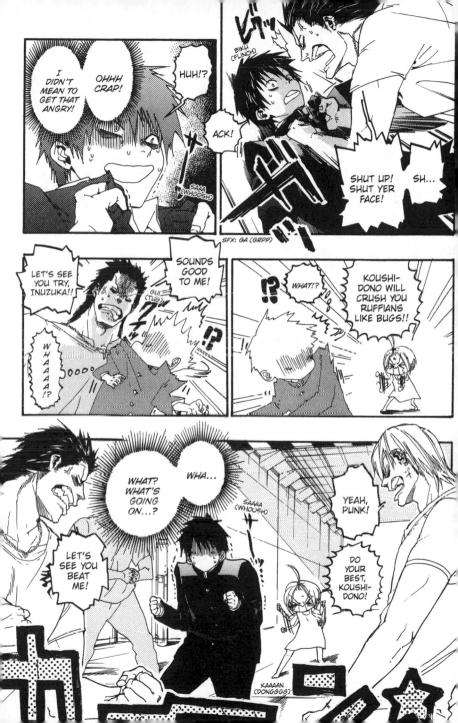

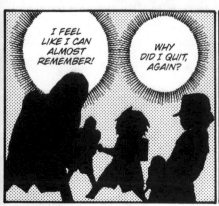

I FEEL LIKE I CAN ALMOST REMEMBER!

WHY DID I QUIT, AGAIN?

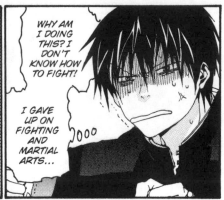

WHY AM I DOING THIS? I DON'T KNOW HOW TO FIGHT!

I GAVE UP ON FIGHTING AND MARTIAL ARTS...

SFX: ZUKI (THUMP)

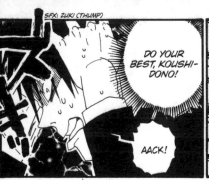

DO YOUR BEST, KOUSHI-DONO!

AACK!

SFX: BIKU (FLINCH)

DO YOUR BEST, KOUSHI-DONO!

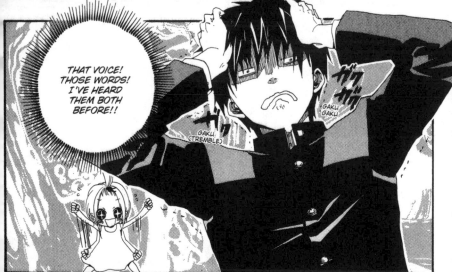

THAT VOICE! THOSE WORDS! I'VE HEARD THEM BOTH BEFORE!!

GAKU GAKU

GAKU (TREMBLE)

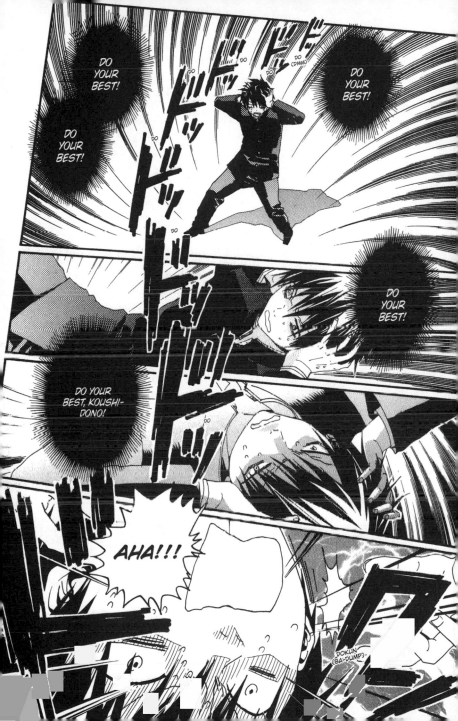

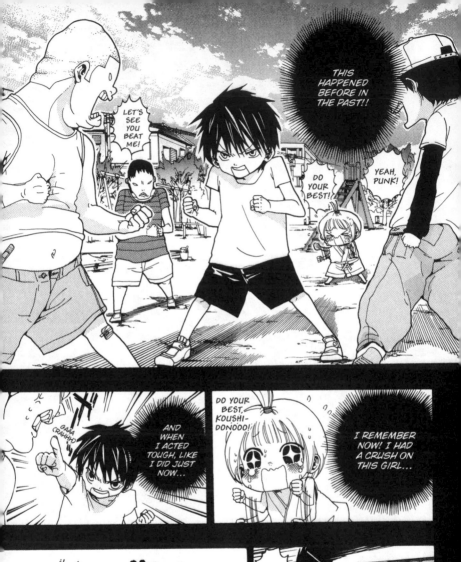
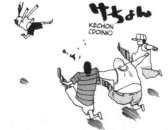
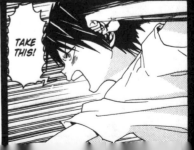

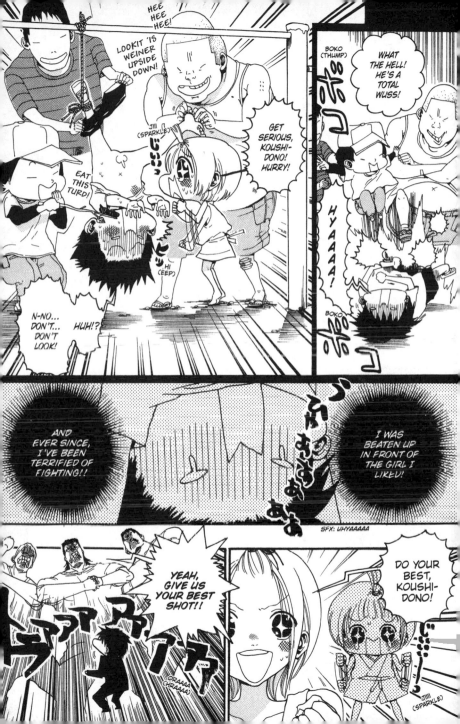

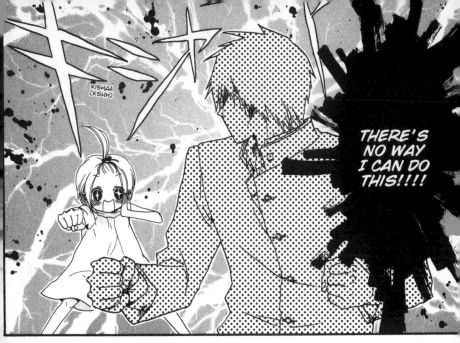

KISHAA (KSHH)

THERE'S NO WAY I CAN DO THIS!!!!

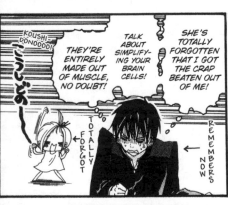

KOUSHI-DONOOOO!

THEY'RE ENTIRELY MADE OUT OF MUSCLE, NO DOUBT!

TALK ABOUT SIMPLIFY-ING YOUR BRAIN CELLS!

SHE'S TOTALLY FORGOTTEN THAT I GOT THE CRAP BEATEN OUT OF ME!

TOTALLY FORGOT ←

→ REMEMBERS NOW

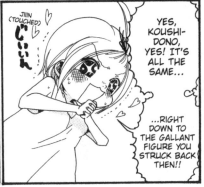

JIIN (TOUCHED)

YES, KOUSHI-DONO, YES! IT'S ALL THE SAME...

...RIGHT DOWN TO THE GALLANT FIGURE YOU STRUCK BACK THEN!!

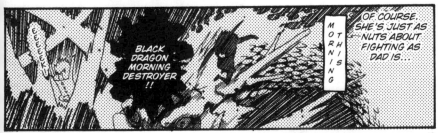

EEEEEK

BLACK DRAGON MORNING DESTROYER !!

MORNING THIS

OF COURSE. SHE'S JUST AS NUTS ABOUT FIGHTING AS DAD IS...

40

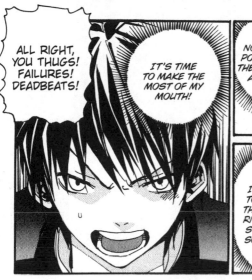

ALL RIGHT, YOU THUGS! FAILURES! DEADBEATS!

IT'S TIME TO MAKE THE MOST OF MY MOUTH!

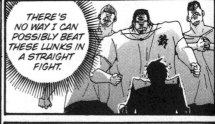

THERE'S NO WAY I CAN POSSIBLY BEAT THESE LUNKS IN A STRAIGHT FIGHT.

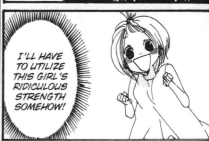

I'LL HAVE TO UTILIZE THIS GIRL'S RIDICULOUS STRENGTH SOMEHOW!

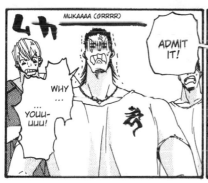

MUKAAAA (GRRRR)

WHY... ...YOUU-UUU!

ADMIT IT!

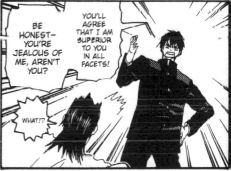

BE HONEST—YOU'RE JEALOUS OF ME, AREN'T YOU?

YOU'LL AGREE THAT I AM SUPERIOR TO YOU IN ALL FACETS!

WHAT!?

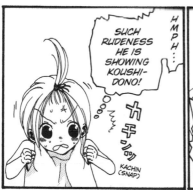

SUCH RUDENESS HE IS SHOWING KOUSHI-DONO!

HMPH...

KACHIN (SNAP)

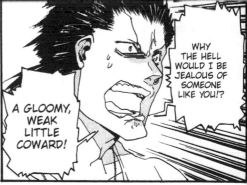

A GLOOMY, WEAK LITTLE COWARD!

WHY THE HELL WOULD I BE JEALOUS OF SOMEONE LIKE YOU!?

41

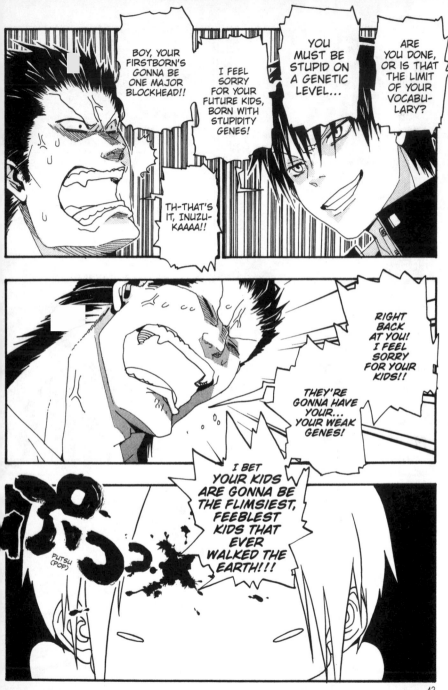

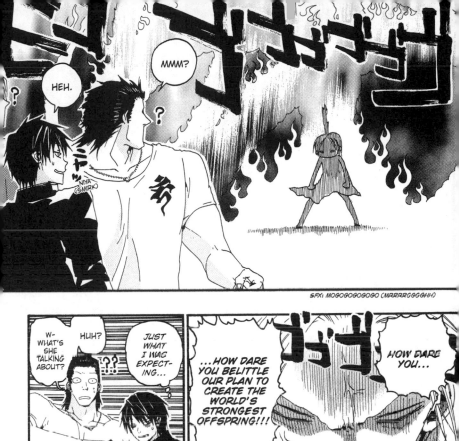

SFX: MOGOGOGOGOGO (MRRRRGGGGHH)

SFX: GAOOOOO (ROAAARRRR)   SFX: DOKI (BADUMP) DOKI

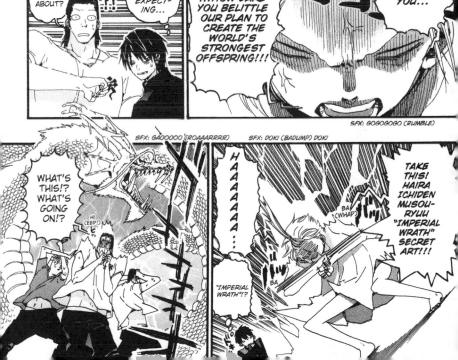

SFX: GOGOGOGO (RUMBLE)

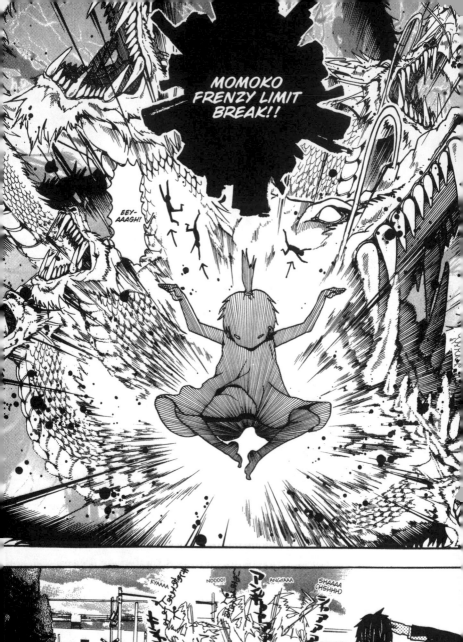

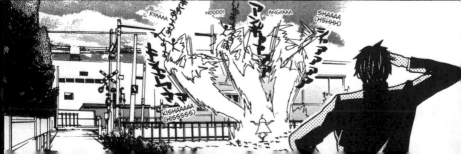

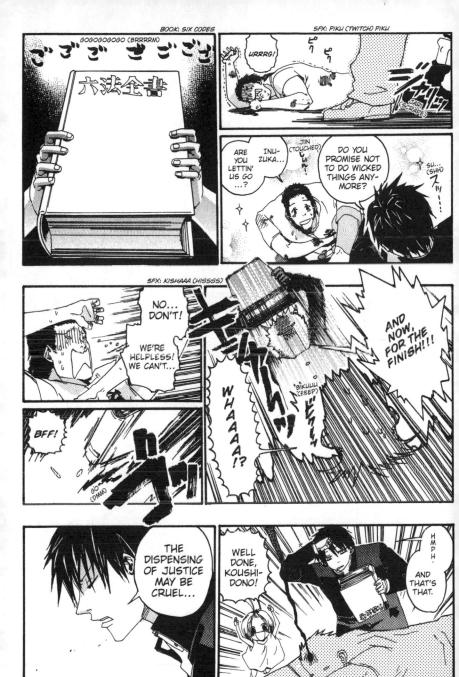

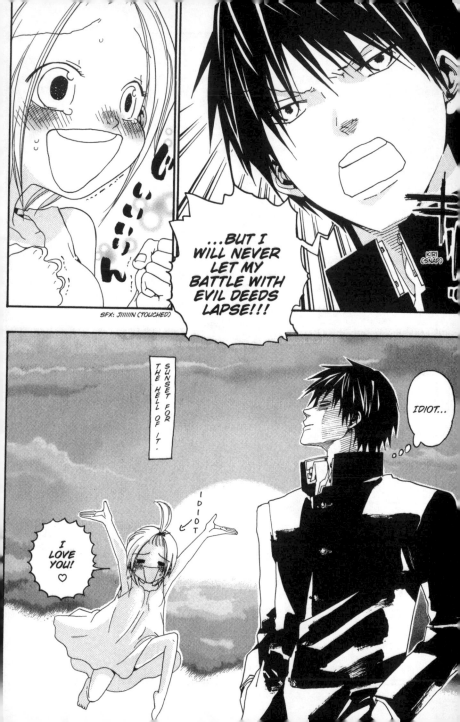

NO, NO! NO MAR-RIAGES!!

AND NOW, THE CEREMONY!

YOUR SPOT

VERY GOOD!!

WE HAVE RETURNED, FATHER-IN-LAW!!

SFX: GARAGARAAA (SHHUNK)

WHY WOULD I NOT!?

YOU ARE STILL WILLING TO UNDERGO RITUAL MATRIMONY WITH THIS PASTY, FEEBLE SON OF MINE?

SAAAA (URRP)

I WASN'T EXPECTING THIS!!

...UNTIL THE DAY KOUSHI-DONO DEEMS ME FIT TO BE HIS WIFE!!

WHAAAT!!?

IN THAT CASE, I WISH TO REMAIN IN THE INUZUKA HOUSEHOLD TO DISCIPLINE MYSELF...

ZA!! (STMP)

AS I HAVE WITNESSED FOR MYSELF THIS VERY DAY...

...KOUSHI-DONO IS EVER AS STRONG AND BENEVOLENT AS I KNEW HIM TO BE!!

...!!

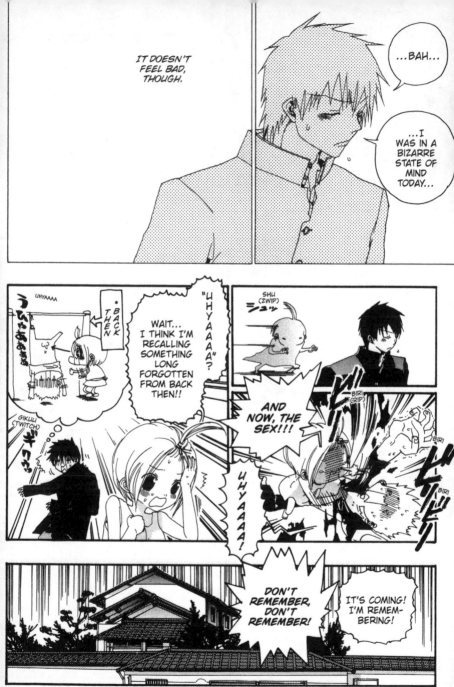

CHAPTER 0. THE STRONGEST FIANCÉE ON EARTH – END

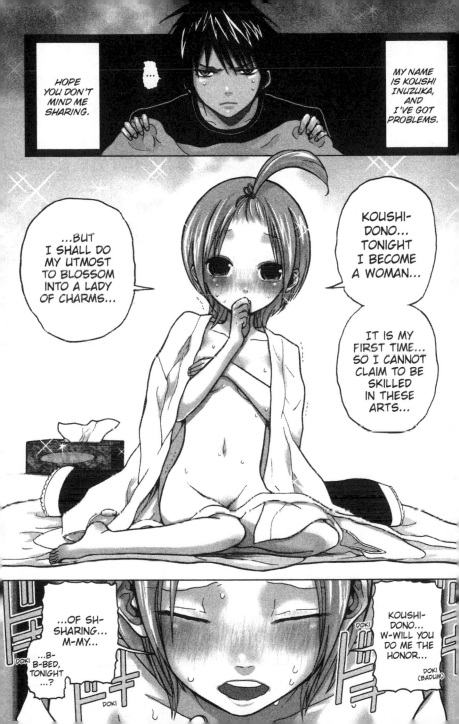

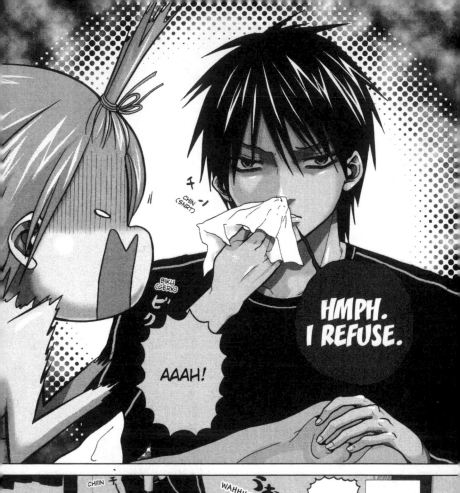

CHIN (SNRT)

BIKU (GERK)

HMPH. I REFUSE.

AAAH!

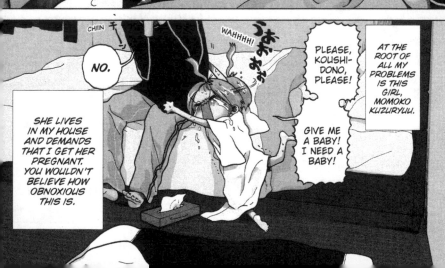

CHIIN

NO.

WAHHHH!

SHE LIVES IN MY HOUSE AND DEMANDS THAT I GET HER PREGNANT. YOU WOULDN'T BELIEVE HOW OBNOXIOUS THIS IS.

PLEASE, KOUSHI-DONO, PLEASE!

GIVE ME A BABY! I NEED A BABY!

AT THE ROOT OF ALL MY PROBLEMS IS THIS GIRL, MOMOKO KUZURYUU.

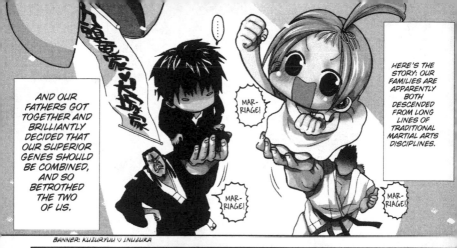

HERE'S THE STORY: OUR FAMILIES ARE APPARENTLY BOTH DESCENDED FROM LONG LINES OF TRADITIONAL MARTIAL ARTS DISCIPLINES.

AND OUR FATHERS GOT TOGETHER AND BRILLIANTLY DECIDED THAT OUR SUPERIOR GENES SHOULD BE COMBINED, AND SO BETROTHED THE TWO OF US.

MAR-RIAGE!

MAR-RIAGE!

MAR-RIAGE!

BANNER: KUZURYUU ♡ INUZUKA

I KNEW HER WHEN I WAS A LITTLE KID, AND THE EXPERI-ENCES I WAS PUT THROUGH ON HER BEHALF HAVE LEFT ME ABSOLUTELY TERRIFIED OF THE THREAT OF VIOLENCE...

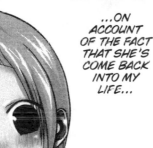

UHYAAAA!

PLUS, THIS GIRL IS TROUBLE. I KNOW FROM EXPERI-ENCE.

WELL, I'M NOT GETTING MARRIED TO HER! I'M JUST A NORMAL PERSON WITH NO INTEREST IN MARTIAL ARTS.

...ON ACCOUNT OF THE FACT THAT SHE'S COME BACK INTO MY LIFE...

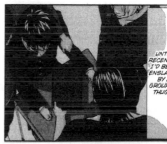

UNTIL RECENTLY, I'D BEEN ENSLAVED BY A GROUP OF THUGS.

?

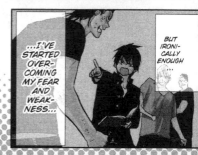

...I'VE STARTED OVER-COMING MY FEAR AND WEAK-NESS...

BUT IRONI-CALLY ENOUGH

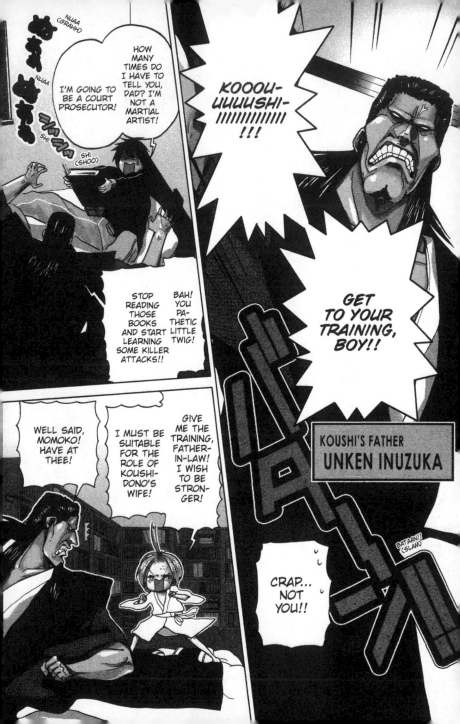

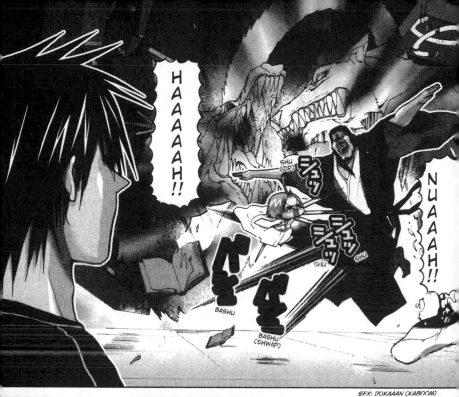

HAAAAAH!!

NUAAAH!!

SHU (ZIP)

SHU

SHU

BASHU

BASHU (SHWAP)

SFX: DOKAAAN (KABOOM)

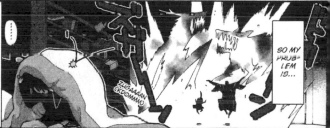

...HOW CAN I LIVE A SANE LIFE UNDER THESE INSANE CONDITIONS?

ZUGAAAAN (KROOMM)

SO MY PROB-LEM IS...

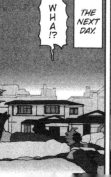

WHA!?

THE NEXT DAY.

YOU'LL SEE, COME THE MORN!

WHAT DOES THAT MEAN?

NOT QUITE!

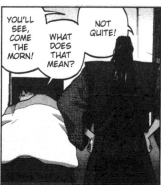

SCHOOL'S THE ONLY PLACE I'M SAFE FROM THESE NUTJOBS.

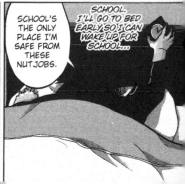

SCHOOL. I'LL GO TO BED EARLY, SO I CAN WAKE UP FOR SCHOOL...

1. THE CLUELESS EXPLODING GIRL

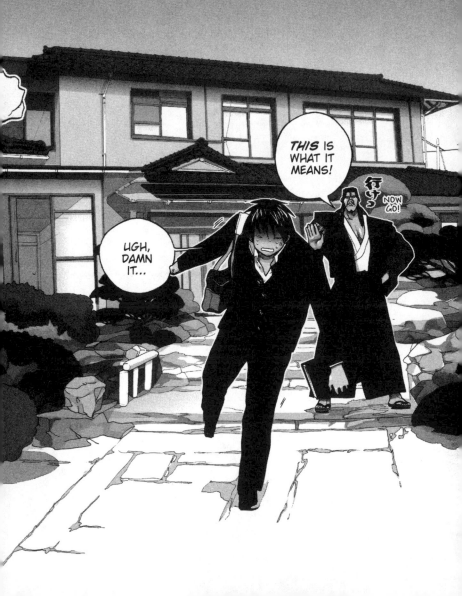

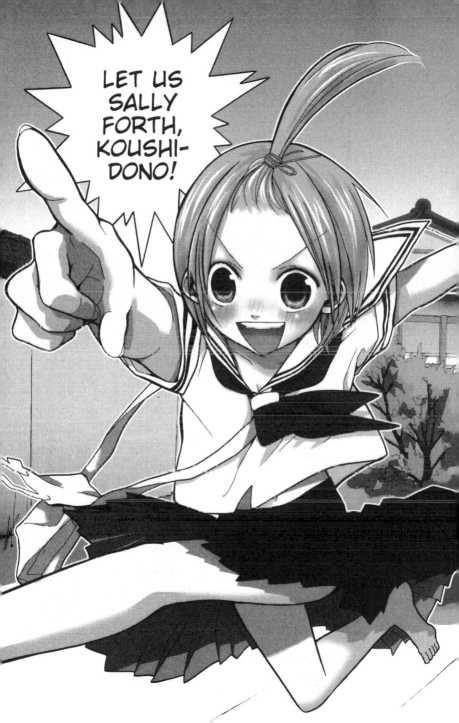

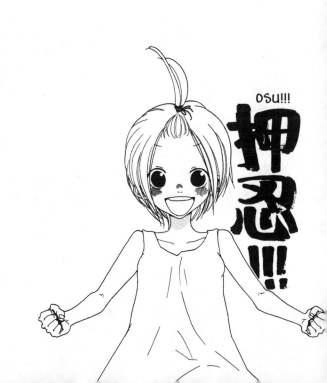

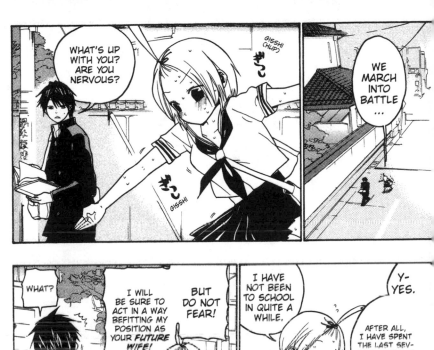

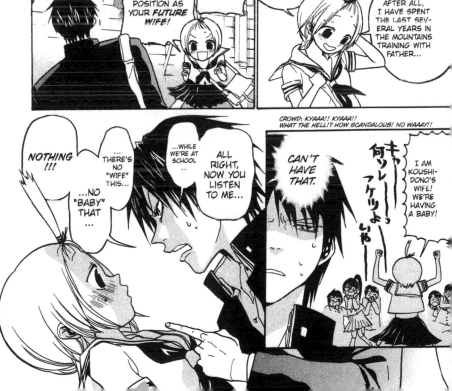

CROWD: KYAAA!! KYAAA!!
WHAT THE HELL!? HOW SCANDALOUS! NO WAAAY!!

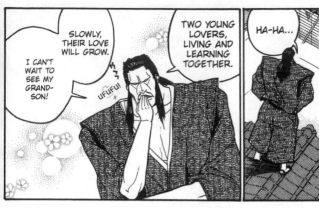

I CAN'T WAIT TO SEE MY GRANDSON!

SLOWLY, THEIR LOVE WILL GROW.

TWO YOUNG LOVERS, LIVING AND LEARNING TOGETHER.

UFUFU!

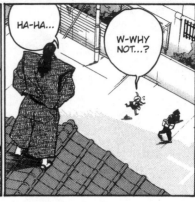

HA-HA...

W-WHY NOT...?

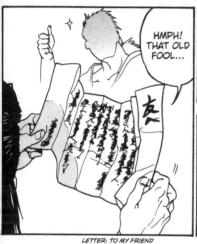

HMPH! THAT OLD FOOL...

LETTER: TO MY FRIEND

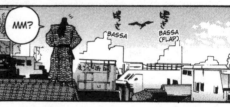

MM?

BASSA

BASSA (FLAP)

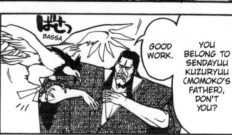

BASSA

GOOD WORK.

YOU BELONG TO SENDAYUU KUZURYUU (MOMOKO'S FATHER), DON'T YOU?

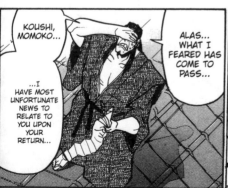

KOUSHI, MOMOKO...

...I HAVE MOST UNFORTUNATE NEWS TO RELATE TO YOU UPON YOUR RETURN...

ALAS... WHAT I FEARED HAS COME TO PASS...

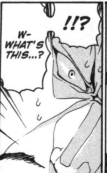

W-WHAT'S THIS...?

!!?

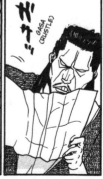

GASA (RUSTLE)

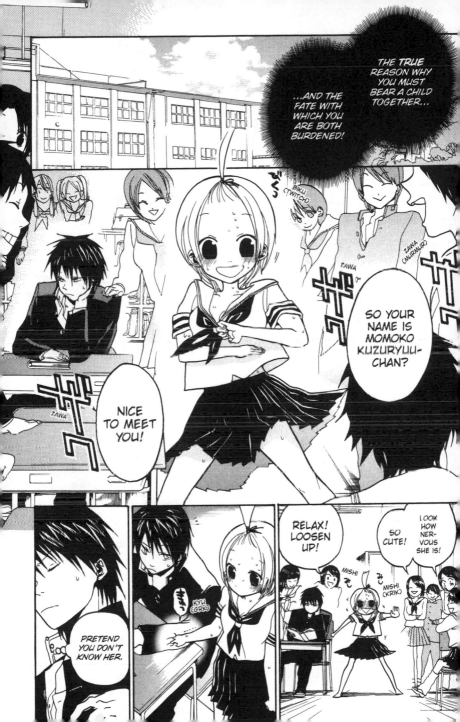

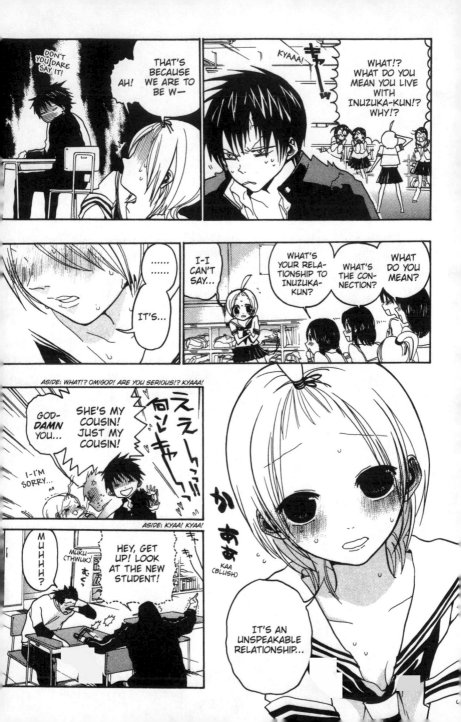

DON'T YOU DARE SAY IT!

AH!

THAT'S BECAUSE WE ARE TO BE W—

KYAAA!

WHAT!? WHAT DO YOU MEAN YOU LIVE WITH INUZUKA-KUN!? WHY!?

......
......

IT'S...

I-I CAN'T SAY...

WHAT'S YOUR RELATIONSHIP TO INUZUKA-KUN?

WHAT'S THE CONNECTION?

WHAT DO YOU MEAN?

ASIDE: WHAT!? OMIGOD! ARE YOU SERIOUS!? KYAAA!

GOD-DAMN YOU...

SHE'S MY COUSIN! JUST MY COUSIN!

I-I'M SORRY...

ASIDE: KYAAA! KYAAA!

MUHHH?

MUKU (THWLIK)

HEY, GET UP! LOOK AT THE NEW STUDENT!

KAA (BLUSH)

IT'S AN UNSPEAKABLE RELATIONSHIP...

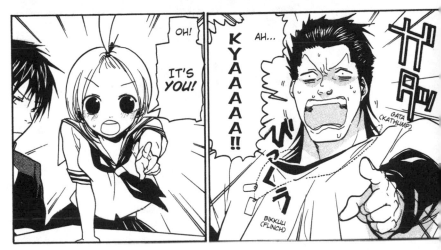

OH!

IT'S YOU!

AH...

KYAAAAA!!

GATA (KATHUMP)

BIKKURI (FLINCH)

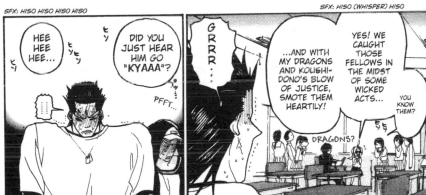

HEE HEE HEE...

DID YOU JUST HEAR HIM GO "KYAAA"?

PFFT...

GRRR...

...AND WITH MY DRAGONS AND KOUSHI-DONO'S BLOW OF JUSTICE, SMOTE THEM HEARTILY!

YES! WE CAUGHT THOSE FELLOWS IN THE MIDST OF SOME WICKED ACTS...

YOU KNOW THEM?

DRAGONS?

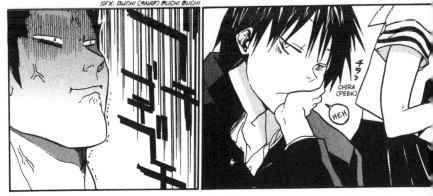

CHIRA (PEEK)

HEH

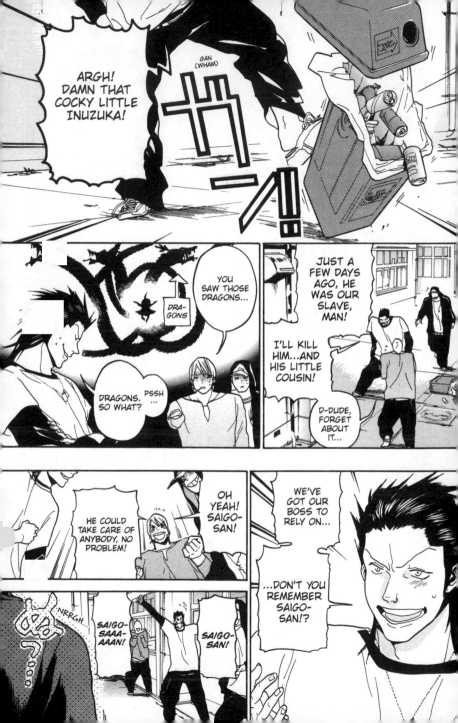

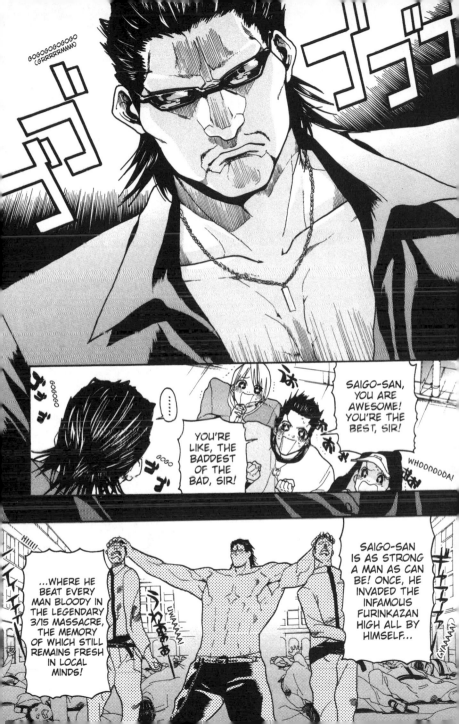

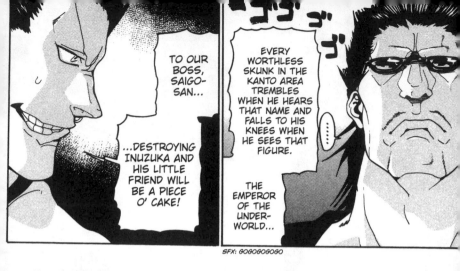

TO OUR BOSS, SAIGO-SAN...

...DESTROYING INUZUKA AND HIS LITTLE FRIEND WILL BE A PIECE O' CAKE!

EVERY WORTHLESS SKUNK IN THE KANTO AREA TREMBLES WHEN HE HEARS THAT NAME AND FALLS TO HIS KNEES WHEN HE SEES THAT FIGURE.

THE EMPEROR OF THE UNDER-WORLD...

SFX: GOGOGOGOGO

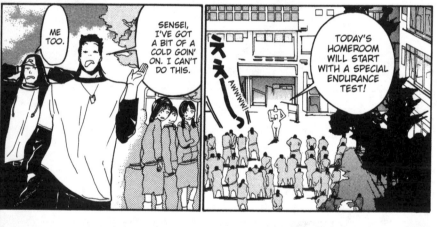

ME TOO.

SENSEI, I'VE GOT A BIT OF A COLD GOIN' ON. I CAN'T DO THIS.

TODAY'S HOMEROOM WILL START WITH A SPECIAL ENDURANCE TEST!

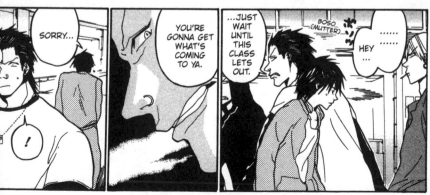

SORRY...

YOU'RE GONNA GET WHAT'S COMING TO YA.

...JUST WAIT UNTIL THIS CLASS LETS OUT.

BOSO (MUTTER)

HEY...

......
......

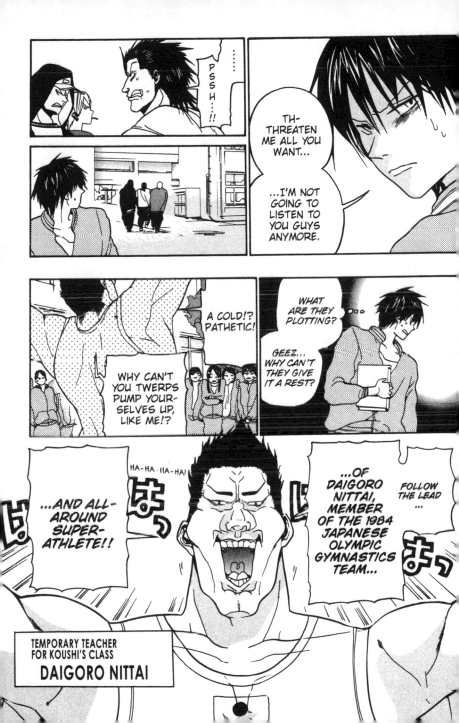

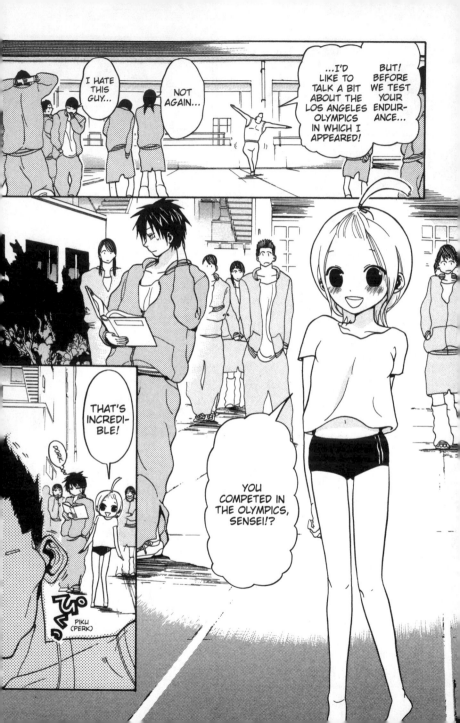

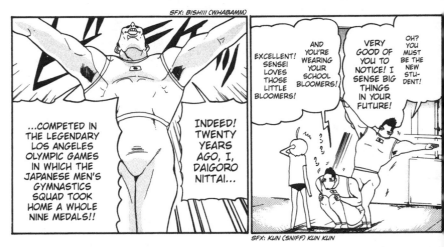

...COMPETED IN THE LEGENDARY LOS ANGELES OLYMPIC GAMES IN WHICH THE JAPANESE MEN'S GYMNASTICS SQUAD TOOK HOME A WHOLE NINE MEDALS!!

INDEED! TWENTY YEARS AGO, I, DAIGORO NITTAI...

EXCELLENT! SENSEI LOVES THOSE LITTLE BLOOMERS!

AND YOU'RE WEARING YOUR SCHOOL BLOOMERS!

VERY GOOD OF YOU TO NOTICE! I SENSE BIG THINGS IN YOUR FUTURE!

OH? YOU MUST BE THE NEW STUDENT!

SFX: KUN (SNIFF) KUN KUN

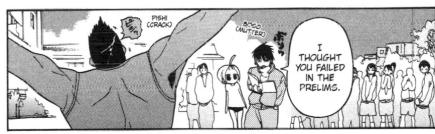

PISHI (CRACK)

BOSO (MUTTER)

I THOUGHT YOU FAILED IN THE PRELIMS.

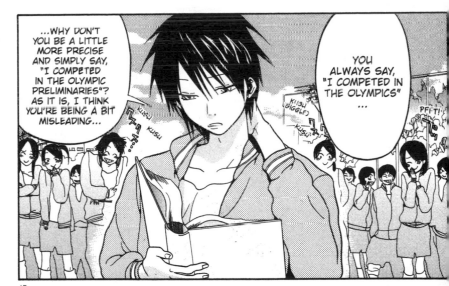

...WHY DON'T YOU BE A LITTLE MORE PRECISE AND SIMPLY SAY, "I COMPETED IN THE OLYMPIC PRELIMINARIES"? AS IT IS, I THINK YOU'RE BEING A BIT MISLEADING...

YOU ALWAYS SAY, "I COMPETED IN THE OLYMPICS"...

KUSU

KUSU (GIGGLE)

KUSU

PFFT!!

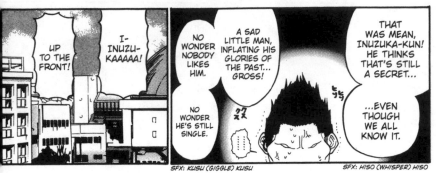

SFX: KUSU (GIGGLE) KUSU

SFX: HISO (WHISPER) HISO

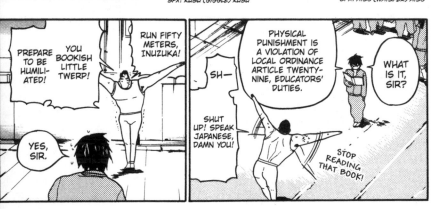

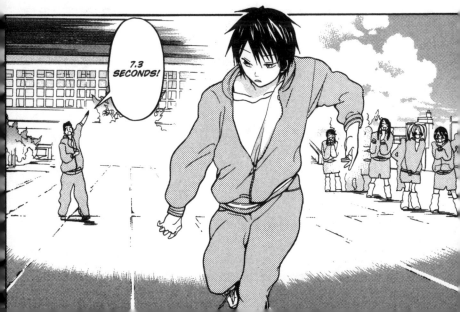

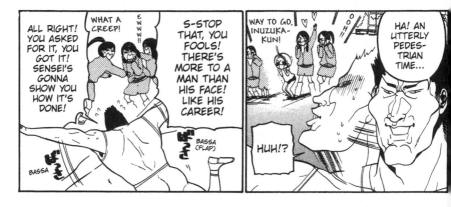

ALL RIGHT! YOU ASKED FOR IT, YOU GOT IT! SENSEI'S GONNA SHOW YOU HOW IT'S DONE!

WHAT A CREEP!

EWWW!!

BASSA

BASSA (FLAP)

S-STOP THAT, YOU FOOLS! THERE'S MORE TO A MAN THAN HIS FACE! LIKE HIS CAREER!

WAY TO GO, INUZUKA-KUN!

OOH!

HUH!?

HA! AN UTTERLY PEDESTRIAN TIME...

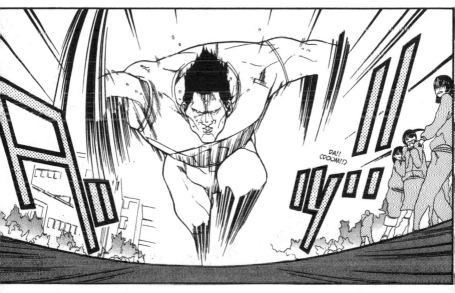

DA!! (DOOM!!)

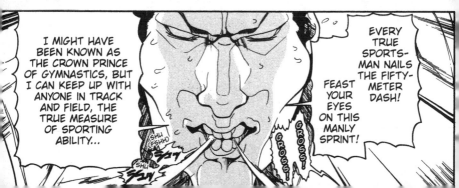

I MIGHT HAVE BEEN KNOWN AS THE CROWN PRINCE OF GYMNASTICS, BUT I CAN KEEP UP WITH ANYONE IN TRACK AND FIELD, THE TRUE MEASURE OF SPORTING ABILITY...

FEAST YOUR EYES ON THIS MANLY SPRINT!

EVERY TRUE SPORTS-MAN NAILS THE FIFTY-METER DASH!

SHU (FSHH)

SHU

GROSS!

GROSS!

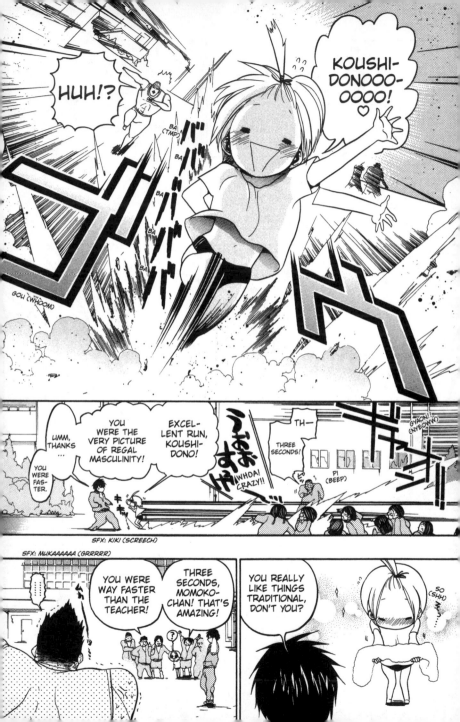

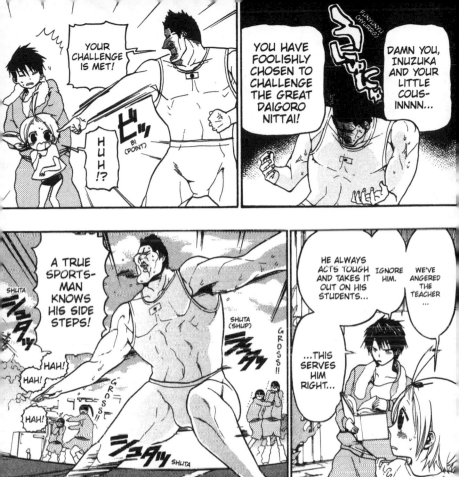

YOUR CHALLENGE IS MET!

HUH!?

BI (POINT)

YOU HAVE FOOLISHLY CHOSEN TO CHALLENGE THE GREAT DAIGORO NITTAI!

FUNYINYI (CHYURG.)

DAMN YOU, INUZUKA AND YOUR LITTLE COUS-INNNN...

A TRUE SPORTS-MAN KNOWS HIS SIDE STEPS!

SHUTA

HAH!

HAH!

HAH!

GROSS!!

GROSS!!

SHUTA (SHUP)

GROSS!!

SHUTA

HE ALWAYS ACTS TOUGH AND TAKES IT OUT ON HIS STUDENTS...

IGNORE HIM.

WE'VE ANGERED THE TEACHER ...

...THIS SERVES HIM RIGHT...

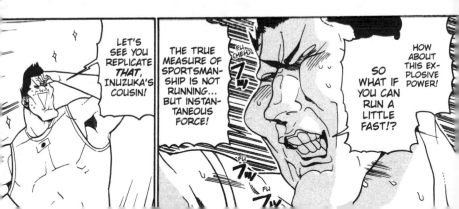

LET'S SEE YOU REPLICATE *THAT*, INUZUKA'S COUSIN!

THE TRUE MEASURE OF SPORTSMAN-SHIP IS NOT RUNNING... BUT INSTAN-TANEOUS FORCE!

FU (CHEH?)

SO WHAT IF YOU CAN RUN A LITTLE FAST!?

HOW ABOUT THIS EX-PLOSIVE POWER!

FU

FU

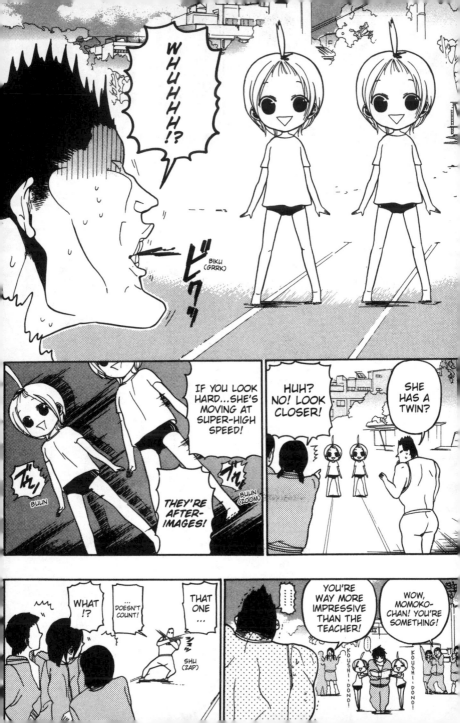

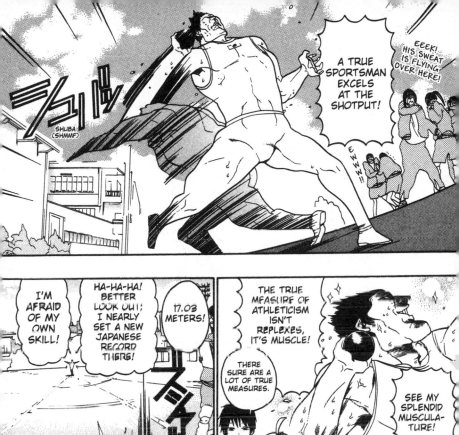

A TRUE SPORTSMAN EXCELS AT THE SHOTPUT!

EEEK! HIS SWEAT IS FLYING OVER HERE!

EWWW!!

SHUBA (SHMMF)

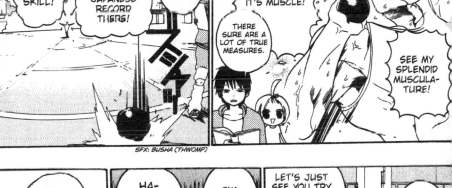

I'M AFRAID OF MY OWN SKILL!

HA-HA-HA! BETTER LOOK OUT; I NEARLY SET A NEW JAPANESE RECORD THERE!

17.03 METERS!

SFX: BUSHA (THWOMP)

THE TRUE MEASURE OF ATHLETICISM ISN'T REFLEXES, IT'S MUSCLE!

THERE SURE ARE A LOT OF TRUE MEASURES.

SEE MY SPLENDID MUSCULATURE!

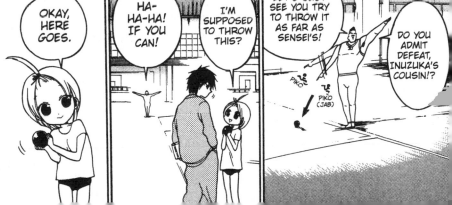

OKAY, HERE GOES.

HA-HA-HA! IF YOU CAN!

I'M SUPPOSED TO THROW THIS?

LET'S JUST SEE YOU TRY TO THROW IT AS FAR AS SENSEI'S!

PIKO

PIKO (JAB)

DO YOU ADMIT DEFEAT, INUZUKA'S COUSIN!?

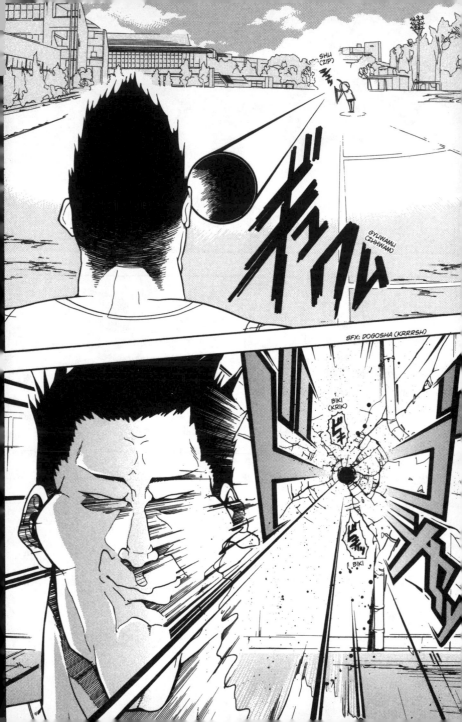

OH! I'M SO SORRY! I'M SO SORRY!

YOU THROW IT PAST HIS RECORD!

YOU'RE NOT SUPPOSED TO THROW IT AT HIM!

NO!

WHOA! DID YOU SEE THAT? MOMOKO-CHAN'S SO BUFF!

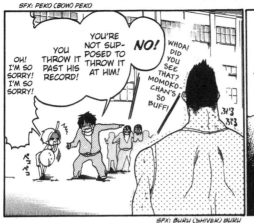

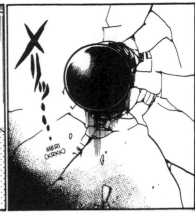

MERI (KRKK)

SFX: BURU (SHIVER) BURU

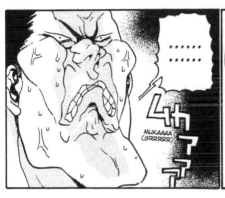

......
......

MUKAAAA (GRRRRR)

UM...

...ARE YOU ALL RIGHT?

CHIRA (PEEK)

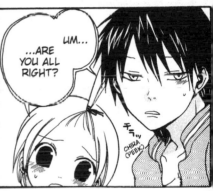

SFX: ZUN (ZMM) ZUN ZUN

WH— WHAT'S HE SO CONFIDENT ABOUT?

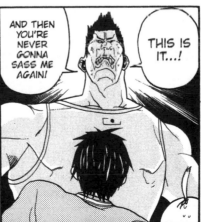

AND THEN YOU'RE NEVER GONNA SASS ME AGAIN!

THIS IS IT...!

ALL RIGHT.

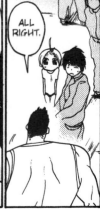

75

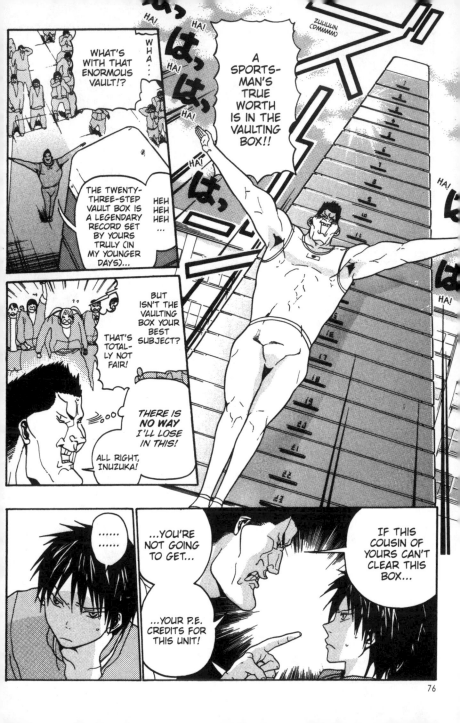

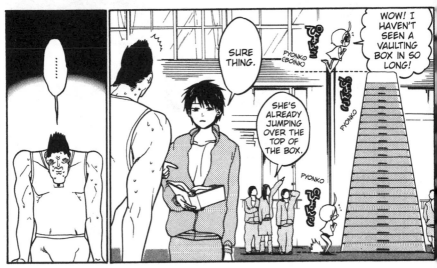

SFX: SHUTATATATA

SFX: SHUTATATATA (SHTUT TUT TUT TUT)

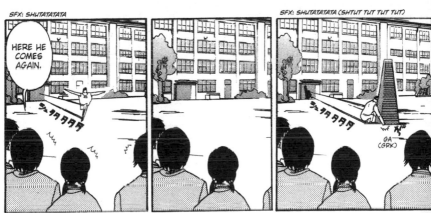

SFX: SU (MMF)

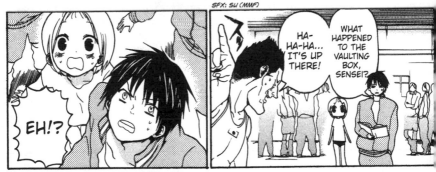

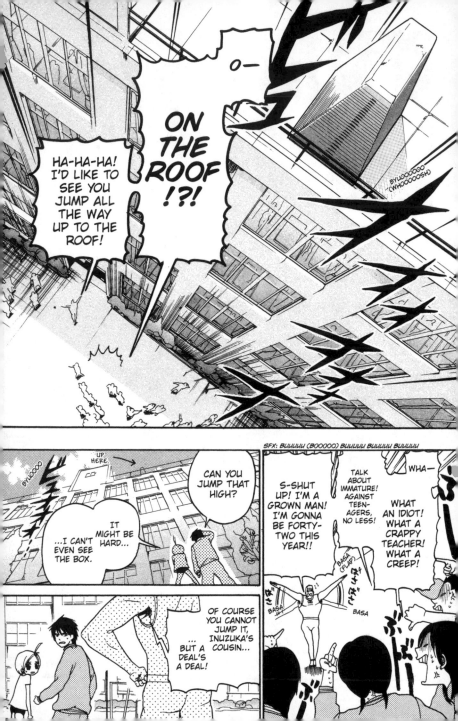

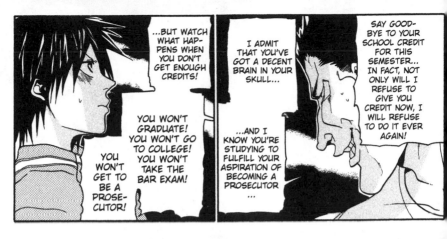

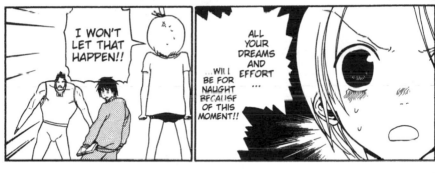

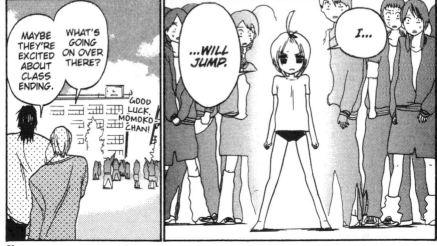

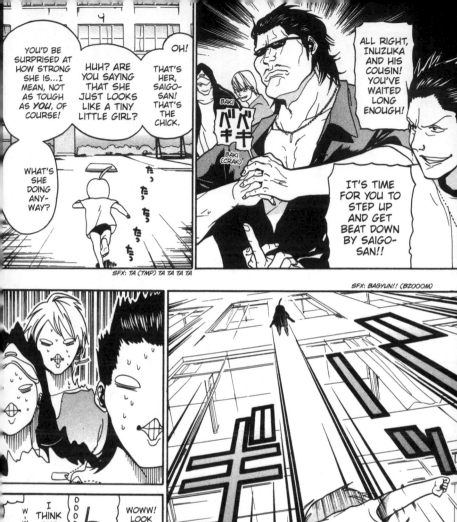

SFX: TA (TMP) TA TA TA TA

SFX: BAGYUN!! (BZOOOM)

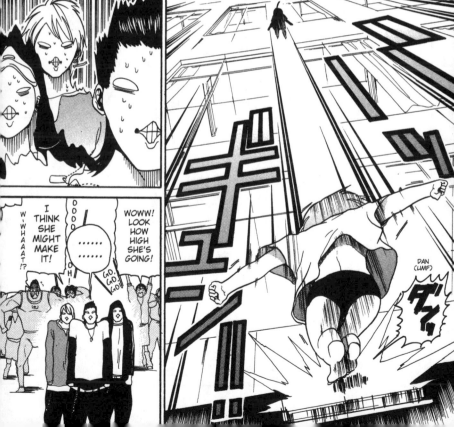

SFX: DAN (LUMF)

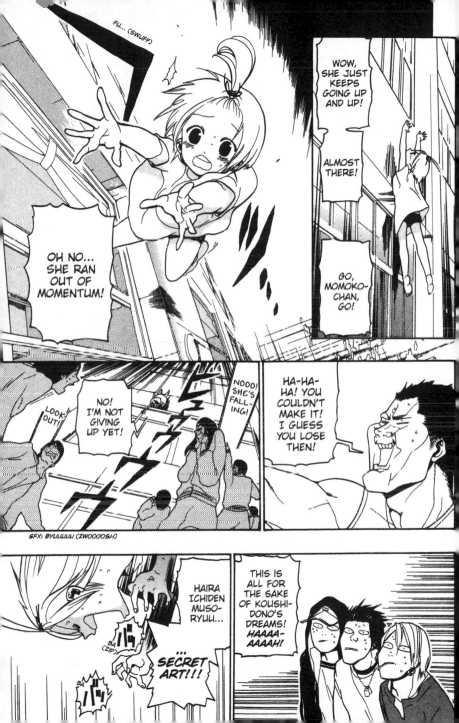

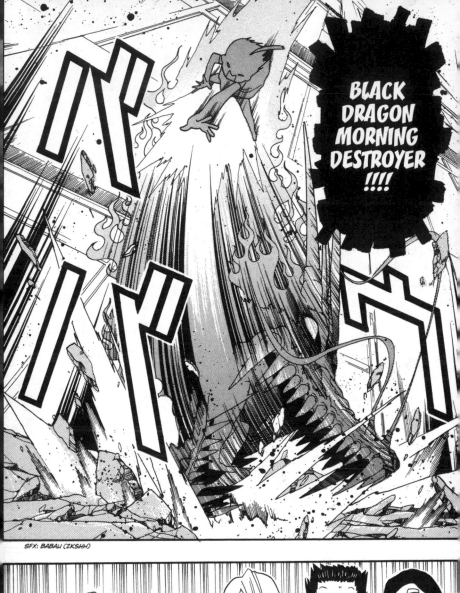

BLACK DRAGON MORNING DESTROYER !!!!

SFX: BABAU (ZKSHH)

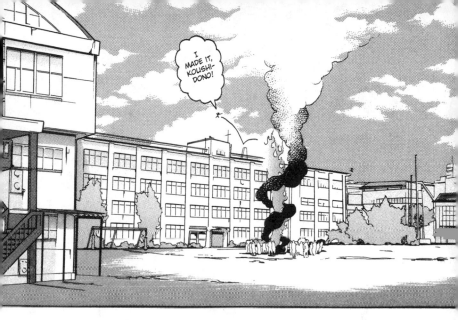

I MADE IT, KOUISHI-DONO!

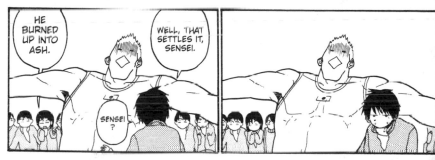

HE BURNED UP INTO ASH.

WELL, THAT SETTLES IT, SENSEI.

SENSEI?

AND ON TOP OF THAT, I'M EVEN INFERIOR IN ATHLETIC ABILITY...

LOOKS LIKE I CAN'T MATCH YOU...

...IN LOOKS OR BRAINS, INUZUKA...

I... I...

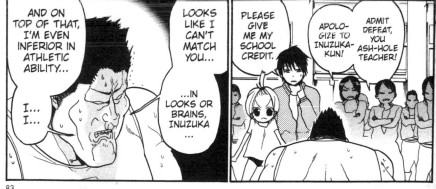

PLEASE GIVE ME MY SCHOOL CREDIT.

APOLO-GIZE TO INUZUKA-KUN!

ADMIT DEFEAT, YOU ASH-HOLE TEACHER!

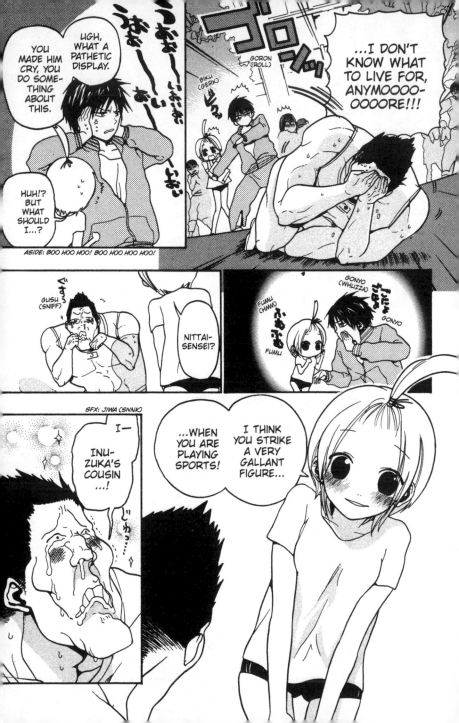

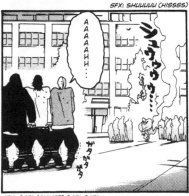

AAAAAHH...

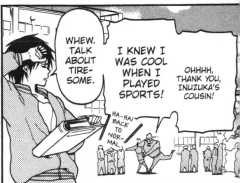

WHEW. TALK ABOUT TIRESOME.

I KNEW I WAS COOL WHEN I PLAYED SPORTS!

OHHHH, THANK YOU, INUZUKA'S COUSIN!

HA-HA! BACK TO NORMAL!

SFX: GATA (SHIVER) GATA GATA

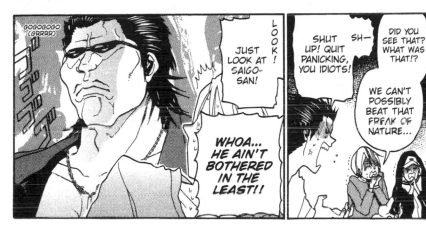

GOGOGOGO (GRRRR)

LOOK!

JUST LOOK AT SAIGO-SAN!

WHOA... HE AIN'T BOTHERED IN THE LEAST!!

SHUT UP! QUIT PANICKING, YOU IDIOTS!

SH—

DID YOU SEE THAT!? WHAT WAS THAT!?

WE CAN'T POSSIBLY BEAT THAT FREAK OF NATURE...

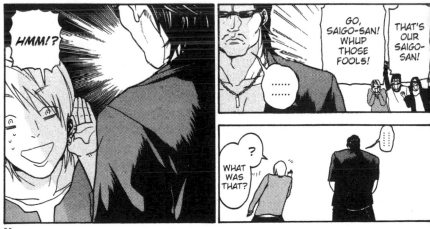

HMM!?

......
......

GO, SAIGO-SAN! WHUP THOSE FOOLS!

THAT'S OUR SAIGO-SAN!

......

WHAT WAS THAT?

?

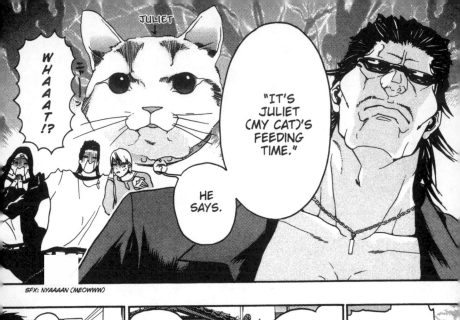

JULIET

WHAAAT!?

"IT'S JULIET (MY CAT)'S FEEDING TIME."

HE SAYS.

SFX: NYAAAAN (MEOWWW)

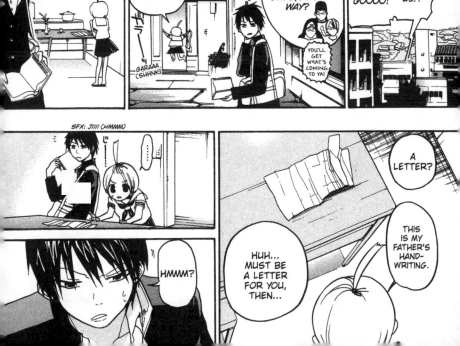

HUH!?

OH.

WE HAVE RETURNED, FATHER-IN-LAW!

GARAAA (SHHNK)

HMM...
WHAT HAPPENED TO THOSE GUYS, ANY-WAY?

YOU'LL GET WHAT'S COMING TO YA!

WAIT, SAIGO-SAN! DON'T GOOOO!

B-BUT WHAT ABOUT SAVING FACE FOR US!?

SFX: JIIIII (HMMM)

HMMM?

HUH... MUST BE A LETTER FOR YOU, THEN...

A LETTER?

THIS IS MY FATHER'S HAND-WRITING.

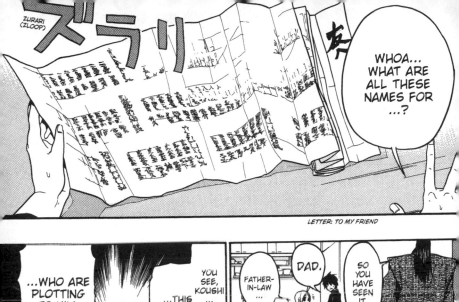

ズラリ
ZURARI
(ZLOOP)

WHOA... WHAT ARE ALL THESE NAMES FOR ...?

LETTER: TO MY FRIEND

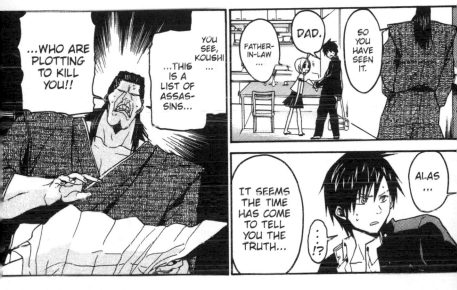

...WHO ARE PLOTTING TO KILL YOU!!

YOU SEE, KOUSHI... ...THIS IS A LIST OF ASSASSINS...

FATHER-IN-LAW...

DAD.

SO YOU HAVE SEEN IT.

IT SEEMS THE TIME HAS COME TO TELL YOU THE TRUTH...

ALAS...

...!?

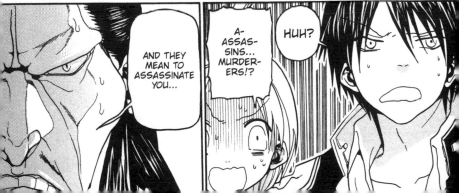

AND THEY MEAN TO ASSASSINATE YOU...

A-ASSASSINS... MURDERERS!?

HUH?

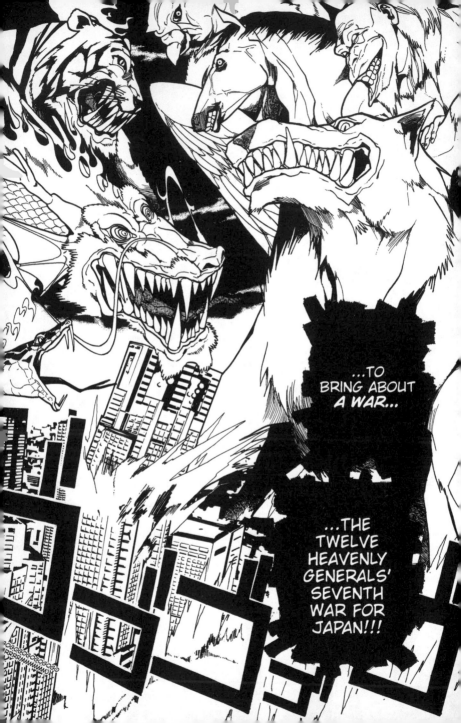

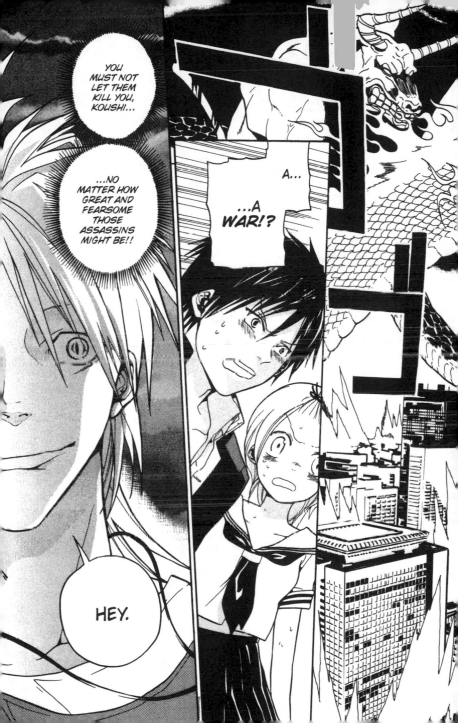

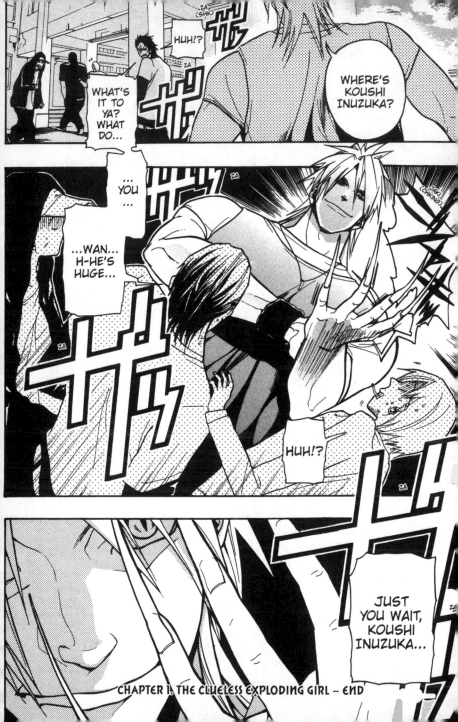

CHAPTER 1: THE CLUELESS EXPLODING GIRL — END

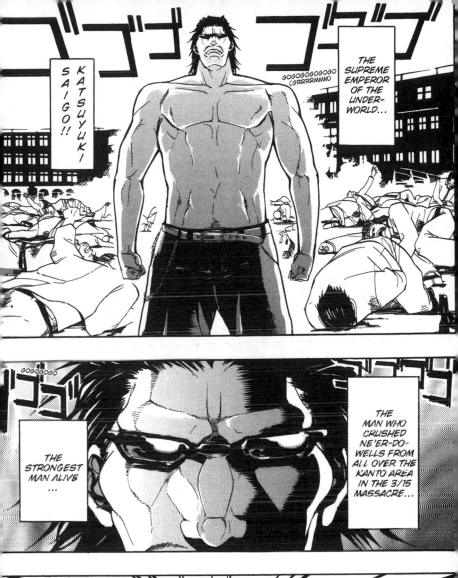

SAIGO!! KATSUYUKI

THE SUPREME EMPEROR OF THE UNDER- WORLD...

GOGOGOGOGOGOGO (GRRRRRMMM)

GOGOGOGO

THE STRONGEST MAN ALIVE ...

THE MAN WHO CRUSHED NE'ER-DO-WELLS FROM ALL OVER THE KANTO AREA IN THE 3/15 MASSACRE...

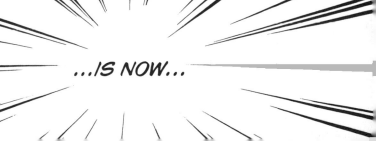

...IS NOW...

2. ENTER THE ASSASSIN

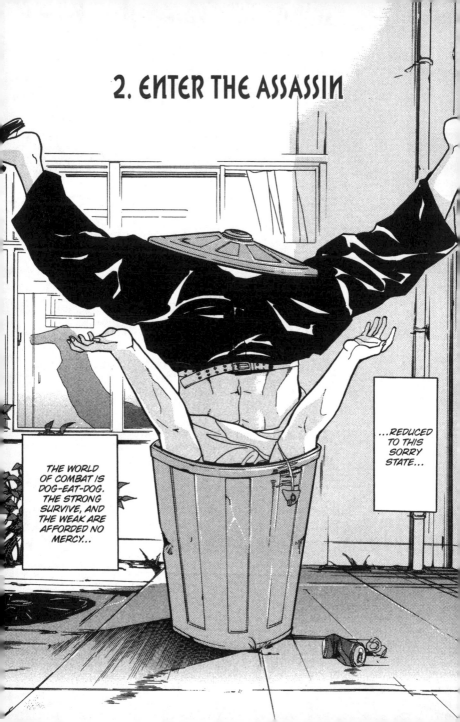

THE WORLD OF COMBAT IS DOG-EAT-DOG. THE STRONG SURVIVE, AND THE WEAK ARE AFFORDED NO MERCY...

...REDUCED TO THIS SORRY STATE...

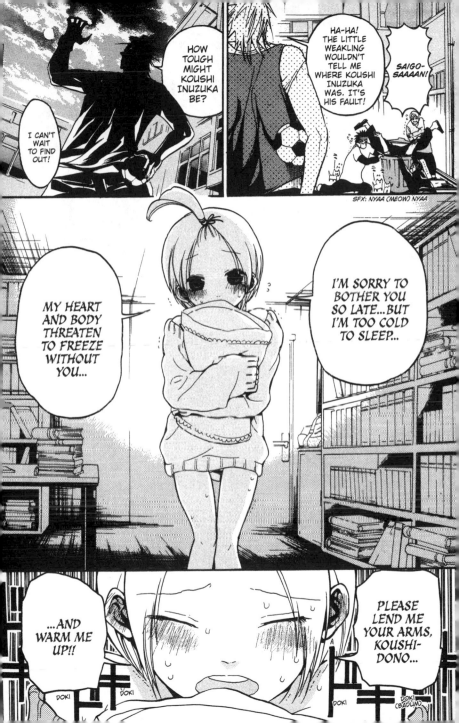

SFX: NYAA (MEOW) NYAA

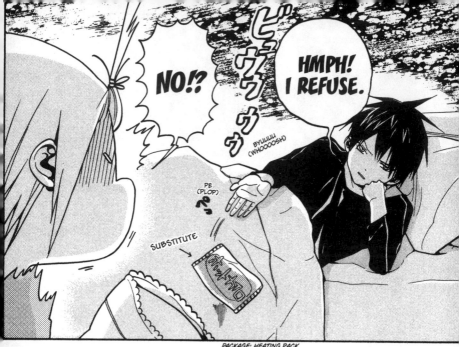

NO!?

HMPH! I REFUSE.

ビゥゥゥ BYUUUU (WHOOOOSH)

PE (PLOP)

SUBSTITUTE

PACKAGE: HEATING PACK

ABOUT THAT, KOUSHI-DONO!

TAKE A HINT. MY LIFE IS IN DANGER, YOU KNOW.

HAVE YOU SEEN MY DAD? I WANT TO KNOW ABOUT THIS GENERAL SOMETHING-OR-OTHER WAR...

HE DIDN'T GIVE ME A FULL EXPLANATION...

OH, BE QUIET.

YOU ARE A COLD MAN...

PACK

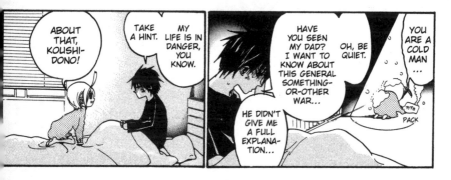

THE HEAVENLY GENERALS' WAR MUST HAVE SOME CONNECTION TO THIS.

APPARENTLY, WITHIN JAPAN THERE ARE TWELVE MARTIAL ARTS FAMILIES, INCLUDING INUZUKA AND KUZURYUU, ALL DIAMETRICALLY OPPOSED TO ONE ANOTHER.

I HAVE HEARD OF SUCH A THING FROM MY FATHER...

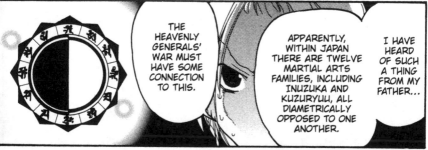

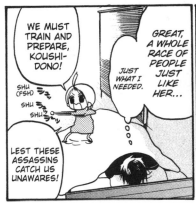

WE MUST TRAIN AND PREPARE, KOUSHI-DONO!

SHU (FSH)

SHU

SHU

LEST THESE ASSASSINS CATCH US UNAWARES!

GREAT, A WHOLE RACE OF PEOPLE JUST LIKE HER...

JUST WHAT I NEEDED.

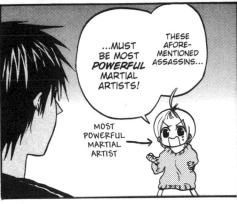

...MUST BE MOST *POWERFUL* MARTIAL ARTISTS!

THESE AFORE-MENTIONED ASSASSINS...

MOST POWERFUL MARTIAL ARTIST

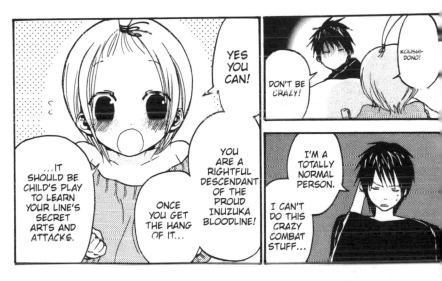

YES YOU CAN!

...IT SHOULD BE CHILD'S PLAY TO LEARN YOUR LINE'S SECRET ARTS AND ATTACKS.

ONCE YOU GET THE HANG OF IT...

YOU ARE A RIGHTFUL DESCENDANT OF THE PROUD INUZUKA BLOODLINE!

DON'T BE CRAZY!

KOUSHI-DONO!

I'M A TOTALLY NORMAL PERSON.

I CAN'T DO THIS CRAZY COMBAT STUFF...

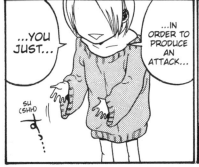

...YOU JUST...

...IN ORDER TO PRODUCE AN ATTACK...

SU (SHH)

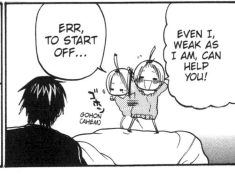

ERR, TO START OFF...

EVEN I, WEAK AS I AM, CAN HELP YOU!

GOHON (AHEM)

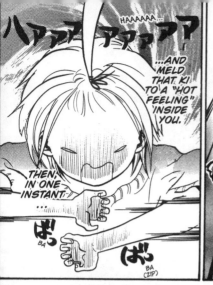

ハァァァァ ァァァァ

HAAAAAA...

...AND MELD THAT KI TO A "HOT FEELING" INSIDE YOU.

THEN, IN ONE INSTANT...

BA

ば BA (ZIP)

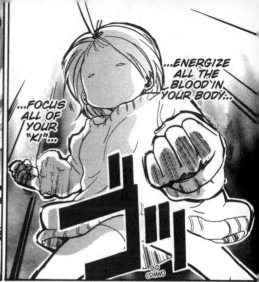

...ENERGIZE ALL THE BLOOD IN YOUR BODY...

...FOCUS ALL OF YOUR "KI"...

ゴッ GO (DMM)

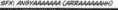

SFX: ANGYAAAAAA (ARRAAAAAHH)

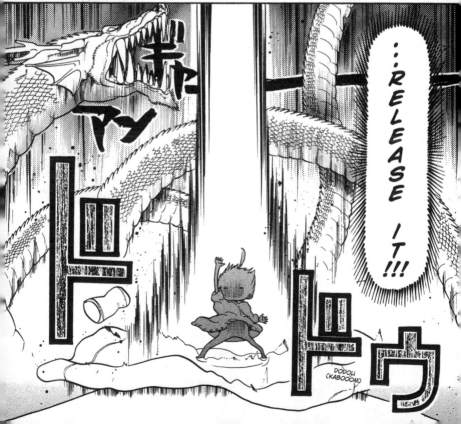

...RELEASE IT!!!

DODOU (KABOOOM)

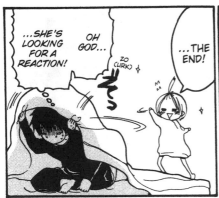

...SHE'S LOOKING FOR A REACTION!

OH GOD...

ZO (URK)

...THE END!

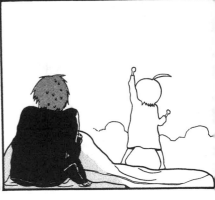

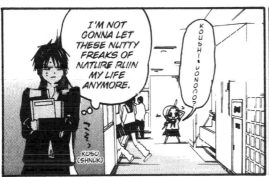

I'M NOT GONNA LET THESE NUTTY FREAKS OF NATURE RUIN MY LIFE ANYMORE.

KOUSHI • IONOOO?

KOSO (SHNLIK)

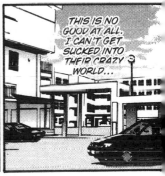

THIS IS NO GOOD AT ALL. I CAN'T GET SUCKED INTO THEIR CRAZY WORLD...

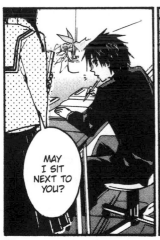

MAY I SIT NEXT TO YOU?

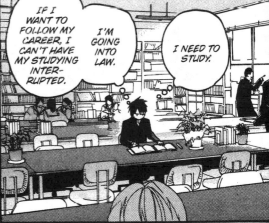

IF I WANT TO FOLLOW MY CAREER, I CAN'T HAVE MY STUDYING INTERRUPTED.

I'M GOING INTO LAW.

I NEED TO STUDY.

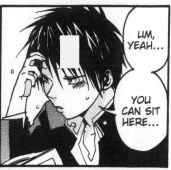

UM, YEAH...

YOU CAN SIT HERE...

CLASS REP...

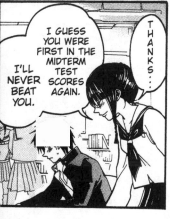

I GUESS YOU WERE FIRST IN THE MIDTERM TEST SCORES AGAIN.

I'LL NEVER BEAT YOU.

THANKS...

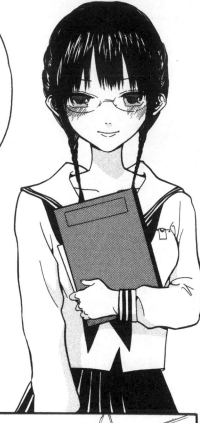

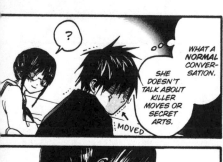

?

WHAT A NORMAL CONVERSATION.

SHE DOESN'T TALK ABOUT KILLER MOVES OR SECRET ARTS.

MOVED

YOU'RE THE MOST SANE PERSON IN MY LIFE.

YOU COULDN'T BE MORE NORMAL, CLASS REP.

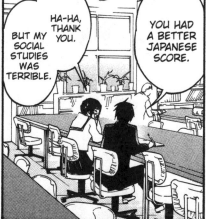

HA-HA, THANK YOU.

BUT MY SOCIAL STUDIES WAS TERRIBLE.

YOU HAD A BETTER JAPANESE SCORE.

I THINK IT'S NORMAL, SMART GIRLS LIKE THIS THAT I'M *REALLY* SUITED FOR...

JUST BEING AROUND YOU SETS MY HEART AT EASE.

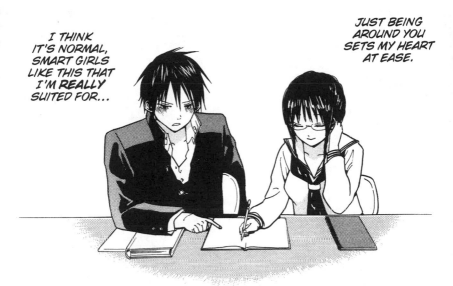

SFX: ZAWA (MURMUR) ZAWA ZAWA

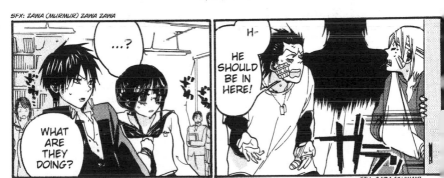

...?

WHAT ARE THEY DOING?

H- HE SHOULD BE IN HERE!

SFX: GARA (SHWAM)

SFX: JAKI (SHWIK)

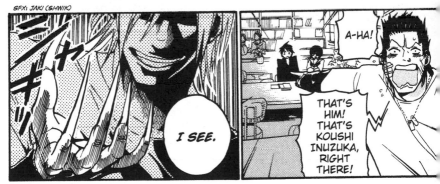

I SEE.

A-HA!

THAT'S HIM! THAT'S KOUSHI INUZUKA, RIGHT THERE!

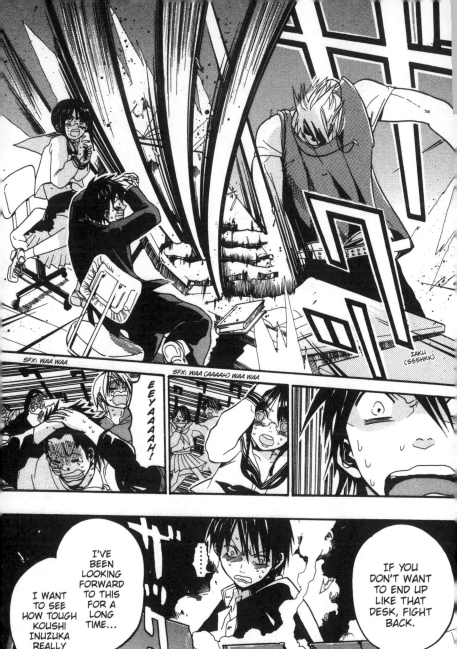

SFX: WAA WAA

ZAKU
(SSSHKK)

SFX: WAA (AAAAH) WAA WAA

EEYAAAAH!

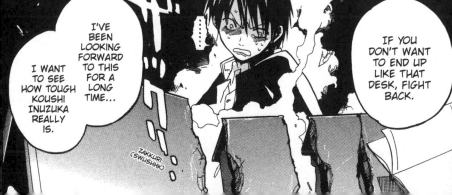

I'VE BEEN LOOKING FORWARD TO THIS FOR A LONG TIME...

I WANT TO SEE HOW TOUGH KOUSHI INUZUKA REALLY IS.

IF YOU DON'T WANT TO END UP LIKE THAT DESK, FIGHT BACK.

ZAKKURI
(SWLSHHK)

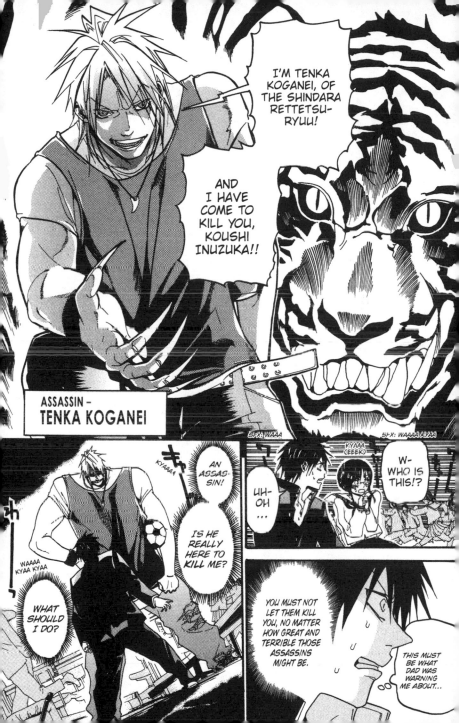

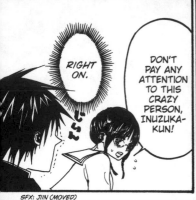

RIGHT ON.

DON'T PAY ANY ATTENTION TO THIS CRAZY PERSON, INUZUKA-KUN!

THIS IS A LIBRARY!

NO... STOP THIS VIO-LENCE!

SFX: JIIN (MOVED)

KOUSHI INUZUKA WILL BE FIGHTING WITH **ME**.

MOVE, GIRL.

BESIDES, OUR SCHOOL IS OFF-LIMITS TO NONSTUDENTS. WE'LL CALL THE POLICE!

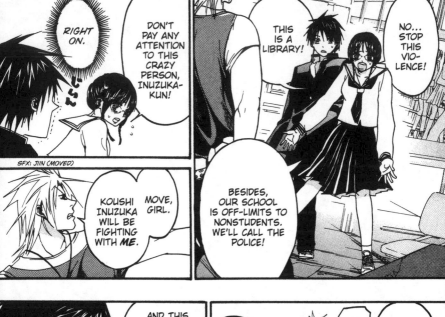

AND THIS "WAR," OR WHATEVER YOU WANT TO CALL IT, HAS NOTHING TO DO WITH ME...

I'M NOT PART OF YOUR WORLD!

YOU PEOPLE JUST DO YOUR THING TO EACH OTHER.

I DON'T INVOLVE MYSELF IN MARTIAL ARTS!

!?

I-I'LL DO NO SUCH THING!

SO SORRY TO DIS-APPOINT YOU.

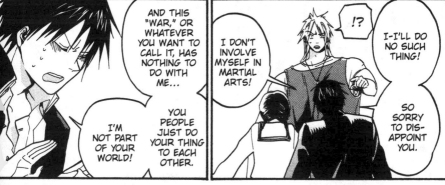

SFX: SHIIIIIN (SILENCE)

.....

MUSU (GRRR)

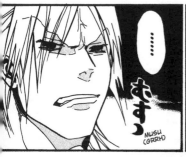

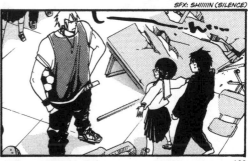

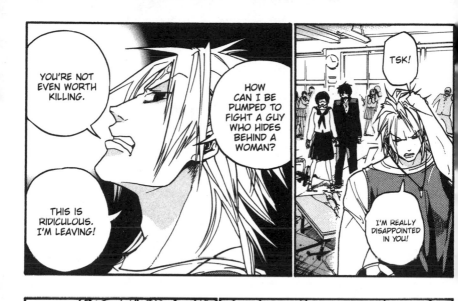

YOU'RE NOT EVEN WORTH KILLING.

HOW CAN I BE PUMPED TO FIGHT A GUY WHO HIDES BEHIND A WOMAN?

THIS IS RIDICULOUS. I'M LEAVING!

TSK!

I'M REALLY DISAPPOINTED IN YOU!

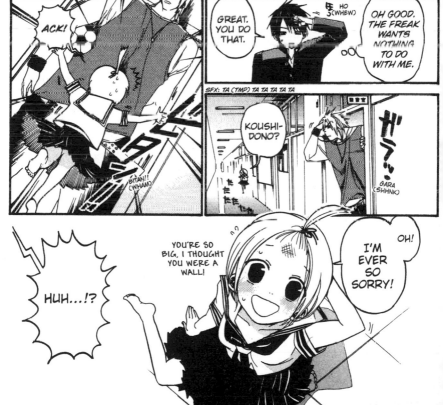

ACK!

BITAN!! (WHAM)

GREAT. YOU DO THAT.

HO (WHEW)

OH GOOD. THE FREAK WANTS NOTHING TO DO WITH ME.

SFX: TA (TMP) TA TA TA TA TA

KOUSHI-DONO?

GARA (SHHNK)

HUH...!?

YOU'RE SO BIG, I THOUGHT YOU WERE A WALL!

OH!

I'M EVER SO SORRY!

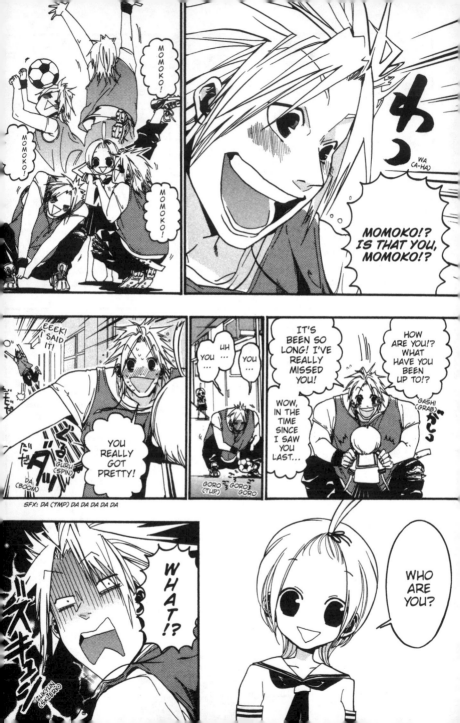

MOMOKO!

MOMOKO!

MOMOKO!

MOMOKO!

WA (A-HA)

MOMOKO!? IS THAT YOU, MOMOKO!?

EEEK! I SAID IT!

GURU (SPIN)

DA (BOOM)

YOU REALLY GOT PRETTY!

UH YOU ...

YOU ...

GORO (TLIP) GORO GORO

IT'S BEEN SO LONG! I'VE REALLY MISSED YOU!

WOW, IN THE TIME SINCE I SAW YOU LAST...

HOW ARE YOU!? WHAT HAVE YOU BEEN UP TO!?

GASH! (GRAB)

SFX: DA (TMP) DA DA DA DA DA

WHAT!?

ZIKYUN (GLARE)

WHO ARE YOU?

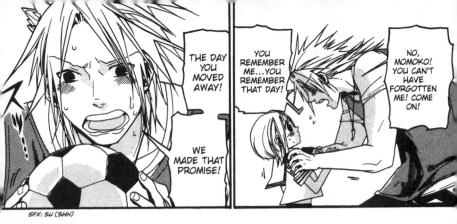

SFX: SU (SHH)

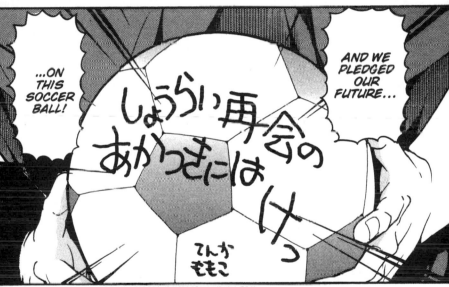

BALL: ON THE DAY WE MEET AGAIN, WE WILL BE M—
TENKA, MOMOKO

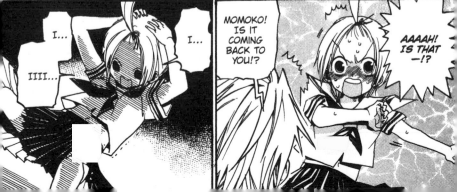

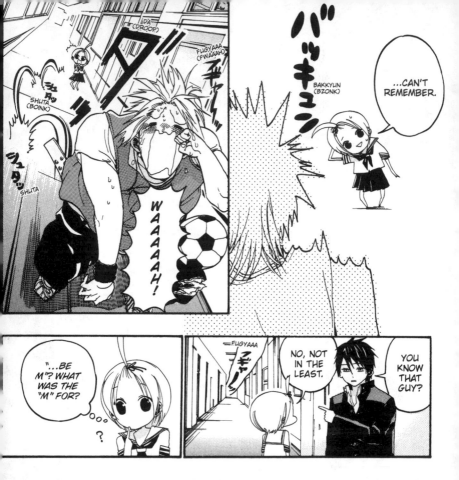

SFX: KARI (SCRATCH) KARI KARI KARI KARI KARI   SFX: KIIN KOON (DING DONG) KAAN KOON

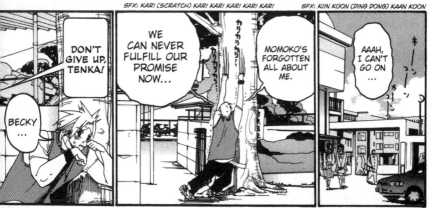

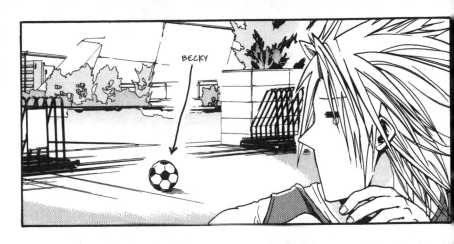

BECKY

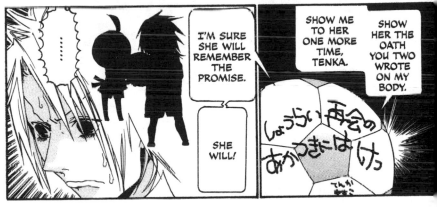

......

I'M SURE SHE WILL REMEMBER THE PROMISE.

SHE WILL!

SHOW ME TO HER ONE MORE TIME, TENKA.

SHOW HER THE OATH YOU TWO WROTE ON MY BODY.

しょうらい再会の
あかつきには
けっ

てんか
ももこ

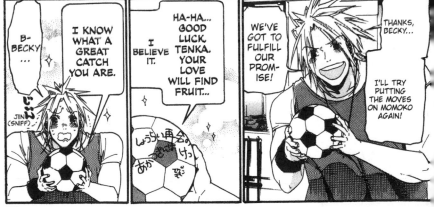

B-BECKY...

I KNOW WHAT A GREAT CATCH YOU ARE.

JIIN (SNIFF)

HA-HA... GOOD LUCK, TENKA. YOUR LOVE WILL FIND FRUIT...

I BELIEVE IT.

しょうらい再会の
あかつきには
けっ

WE'VE GOT TO FULFILL OUR PROM-ISE!

THANKS, BECKY...

I'LL TRY PUTTING THE MOVES ON MOMOKO AGAIN!

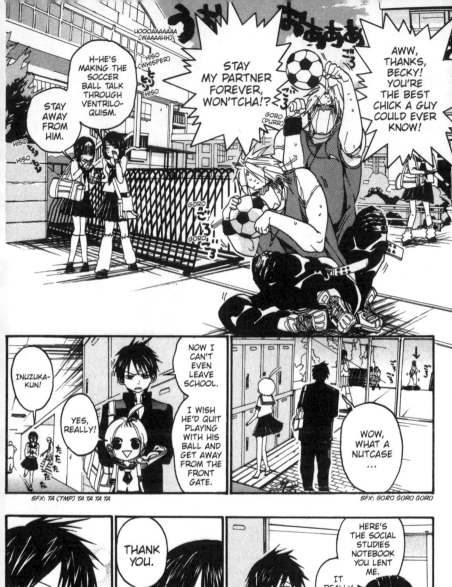

STAY AWAY FROM HIM.

H-HE'S MAKING THE SOCCER BALL TALK THROUGH VENTRILOQUISM.

HISO (WHISPER)

HISO

HISO

HISO

STAY MY PARTNER FOREVER, WON'TCHA!?

GORO (PURR)

AWW, THANKS, BECKY! YOU'RE THE BEST CHICK A GUY COULD EVER KNOW!

UOOOAAAAAAA (WAAAAHHH)

GORO

GORO

INUZUKA-KUN!

YES, REALLY!

NOW I CAN'T EVEN LEAVE SCHOOL.

I WISH HE'D QUIT PLAYING WITH HIS BALL AND GET AWAY FROM THE FRONT GATE.

SFX: TA (TMP) TA TA TA TA

WOW, WHAT A NUTCASE ...

SFX: GORO GORO GORO

THANK YOU.

NIKO (GRIN)

S-SURE...

HERE'S THE SOCIAL STUDIES NOTEBOOK YOU LENT ME.

IT REALLY HELPED A LOT.

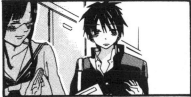

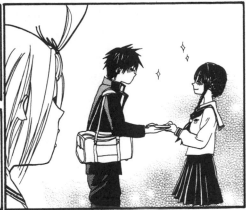

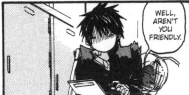

WELL, AREN'T YOU FRIENDLY.

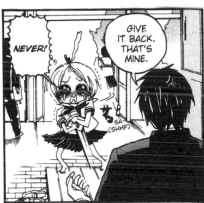

NEVER!

GIVE IT BACK. THAT'S MINE.

SA (SHHP)

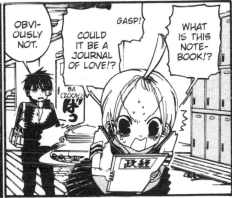

OBVI-OUSLY NOT.

GASP!

COULD IT BE A JOURNAL OF LOVE!?

WHAT IS THIS NOTE-BOOK!?

BA (ZOOM)

NOTEBOOK: SOCIAL STUDIES

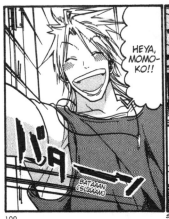

HEYA, MOMO-KO!!

BATAAAN (SLAAAM)

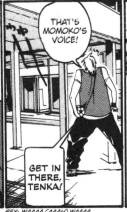

THAT'S MOMOKO'S VOICE!

GET IN THERE, TENKA!

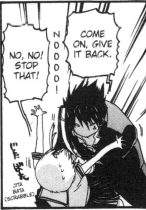

NO, NO! STOP THAT!

NOOOO!

COME ON, GIVE IT BACK.

JITA BATA (SCRABBLE)

SFX: WAAAA (AAAH) WAAAA

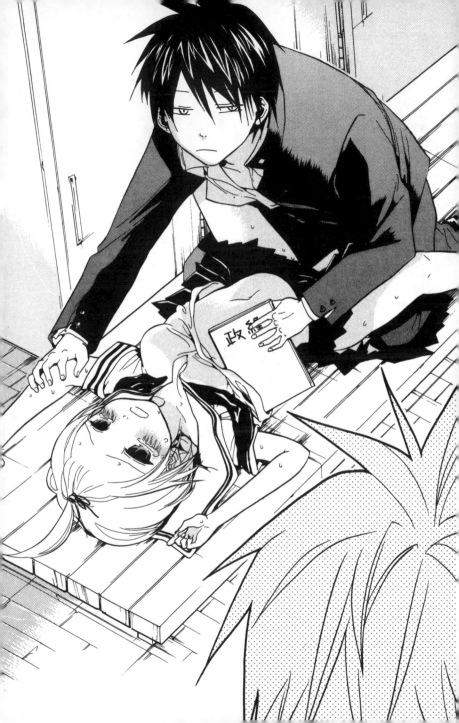

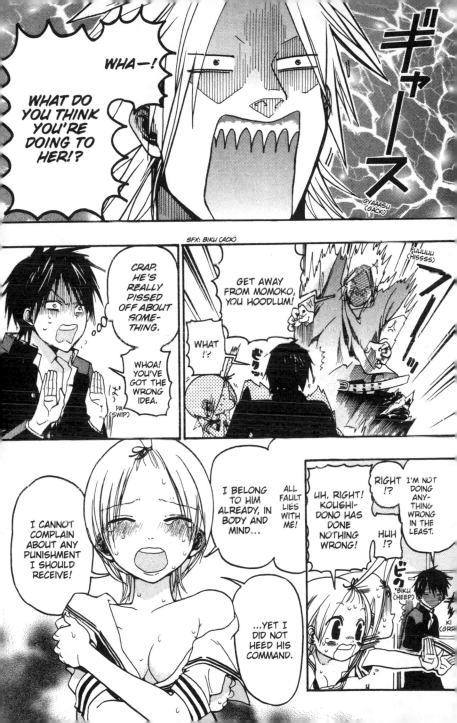

WHA—!

WHAT DO YOU THINK YOU'RE DOING TO HER!?

ギャース

GYAAASU (GACK)

SFX: BIKU (ACK)

CRAP. HE'S REALLY PISSED OFF ABOUT SOMETHING.

WHOA! YOU'VE GOT THE WRONG IDEA.

PA (SWIP)

GET AWAY FROM MOMOKO, YOU HOODLUM!

WHAT !?

ピクッ

FUUUU (HISSSS)

I CANNOT COMPLAIN ABOUT ANY PUNISHMENT I SHOULD RECEIVE!

I BELONG TO HIM ALREADY, IN BODY AND MIND...

ALL FAULT LIES WITH ME!

UH, RIGHT! KOUSHI-DONO HAS DONE NOTHING WRONG!

...YET I DID NOT HEED HIS COMMAND.

RIGHT !?

I'M NOT DOING ANYTHING WRONG IN THE LEAST.

HUH !?

*BIKU (CHEEP)

KI (GRR)

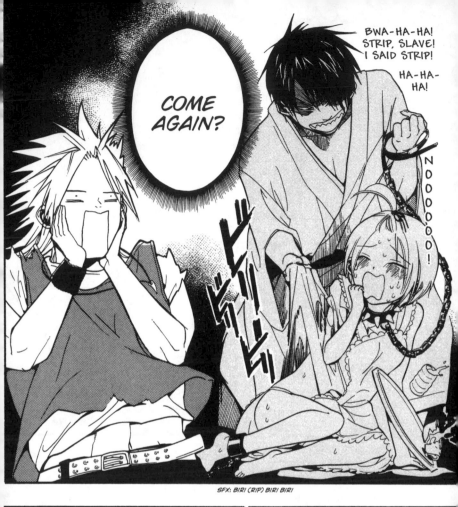

BWA-HA-HA! STRIP, SLAVE! I SAID STRIP!

HA-HA-HA!

NOOOOOOO!

COME AGAIN?

SFX: BIRI (RIP) BIRI BIRI

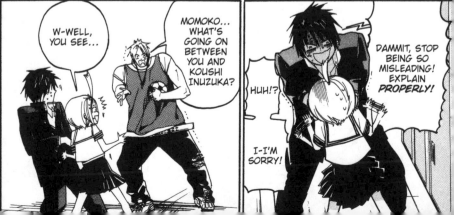

W-WELL, YOU SEE...

MOMOKO... WHAT'S GOING ON BETWEEN YOU AND KOUSHI INUZUKA?

HUH!?

I-I'M SORRY!

DAMMIT, STOP BEING SO MISLEADING! EXPLAIN *PROPERLY!*

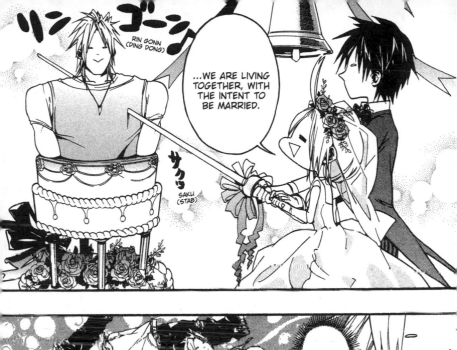

RIN GONN
(DING DONG)

...WE ARE LIVING TOGETHER, WITH THE INTENT TO BE MARRIED.

SAKU
(STAB)

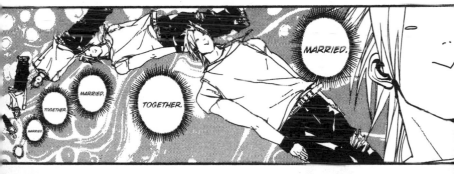

MARRIED.

MARRIED.

TOGETHER.

TOGETHER.

MARRIED

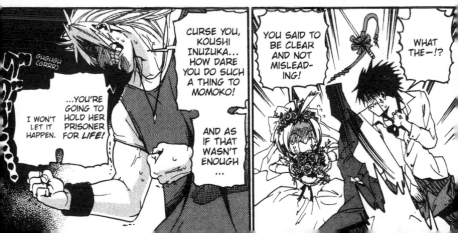

GUGUGU
(GRRR)

I WON'T LET IT HAPPEN.

...YOU'RE GOING TO HOLD HER PRISONER FOR *LIFE!*

CURSE YOU, KOUSHI INUZUKA... HOW DARE YOU DO SUCH A THING TO MOMOKO!

AND AS IF THAT WASN'T ENOUGH...

YOU SAID TO BE CLEAR AND NOT MISLEAD-ING!

WHAT THE—!?

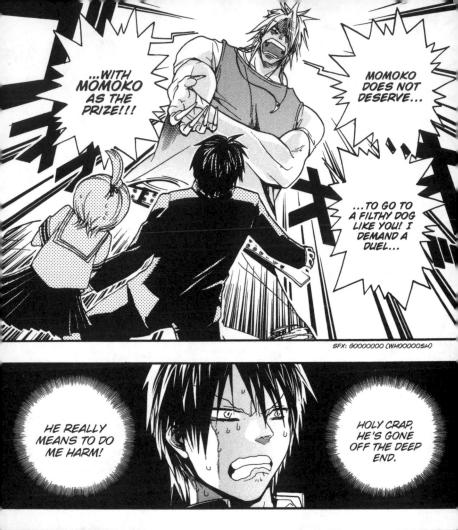

...WITH MOMOKO AS THE PRIZE!!!

MOMOKO DOES NOT DESERVE...

...TO GO TO A FILTHY DOG LIKE YOU! I DEMAND A DUEL...

SFX: GOOOOOOO (WHOOOOOSH)

HE REALLY MEANS TO DO ME HARM!

HOLY CRAP, HE'S GONE OFF THE DEEP END.

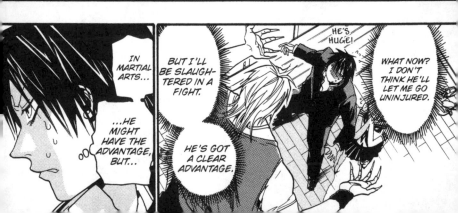

IN MARTIAL ARTS...

...HE MIGHT HAVE THE ADVANTAGE, BUT...

BUT I'LL BE SLAUGHTERED IN A FIGHT.

HE'S GOT A CLEAR ADVANTAGE.

HE'S HUGE!

WHAT NOW? I DON'T THINK HE'LL LET ME GO UNINJURED.

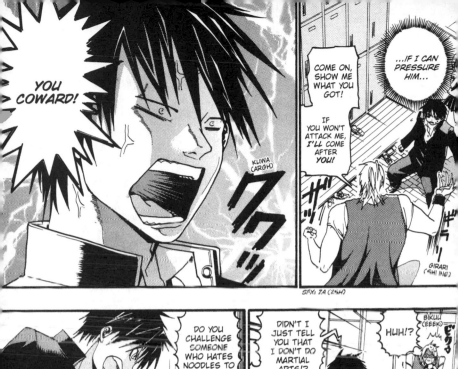
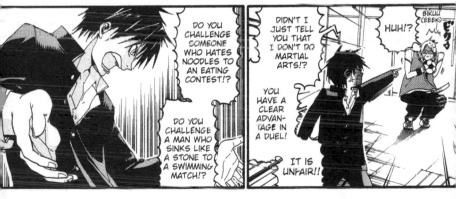
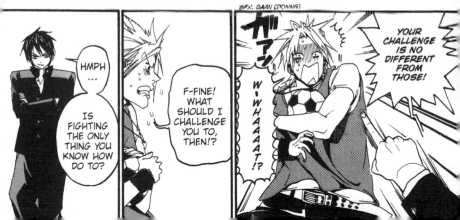

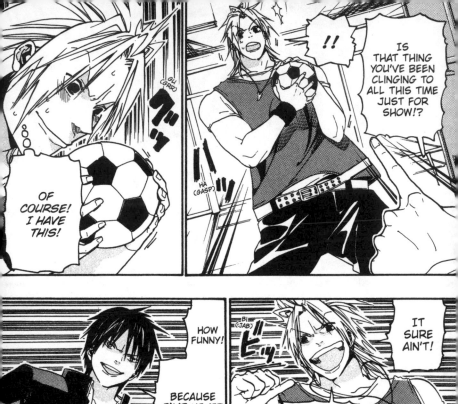

IS THAT THING YOU'VE BEEN CLINGING TO ALL THIS TIME JUST FOR SHOW!?

!!

OF COURSE! I HAVE THIS!

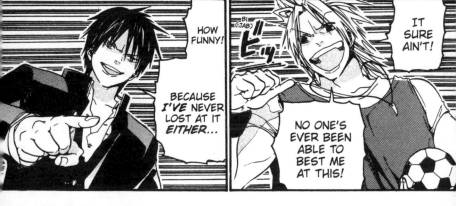

HOW FUNNY!

BECAUSE *I'VE* NEVER LOST AT IT *EITHER...*

IT SURE AIN'T!

NO ONE'S EVER BEEN ABLE TO BEST ME AT THIS!

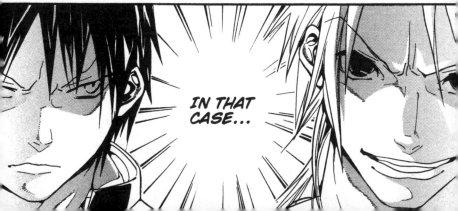

IN THAT CASE...

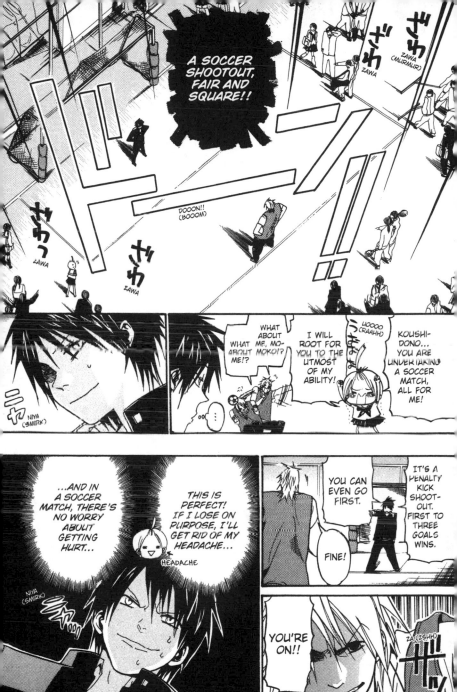

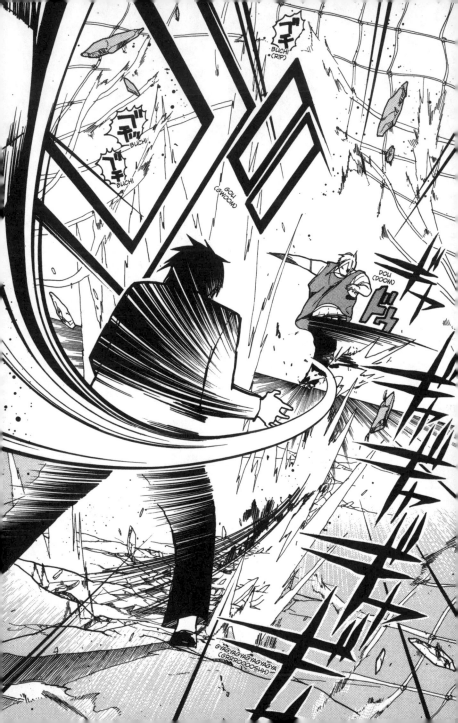

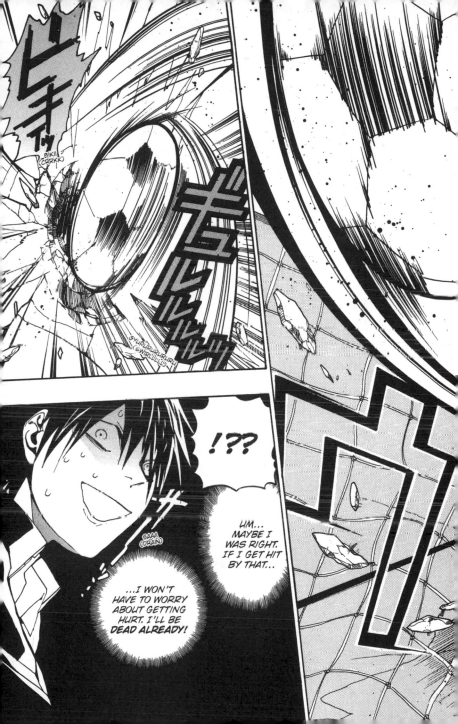

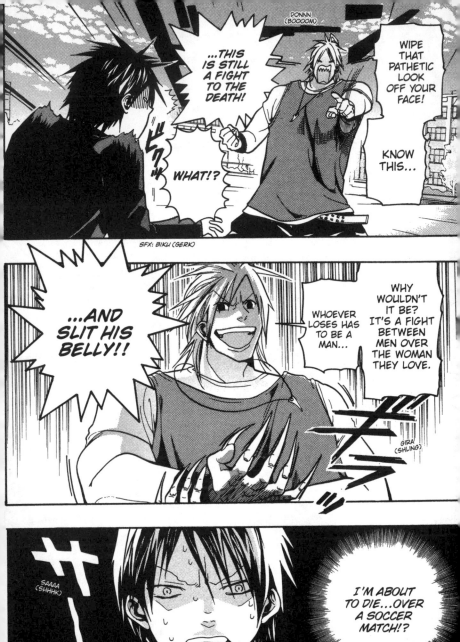

DONNN
(BOOOOM)

...THIS IS STILL A FIGHT TO THE DEATH!

WIPE THAT PATHETIC LOOK OFF YOUR FACE!

KNOW THIS...

WHAT!?

SFX: BIKU (GERK)

...AND SLIT HIS BELLY!!

WHOEVER LOSES HAS TO BE A MAN...

WHY WOULDN'T IT BE? IT'S A FIGHT BETWEEN MEN OVER THE WOMAN THEY LOVE.

GIRA (SHLING)

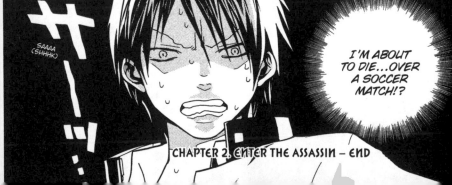

SAAAA (SHHHK)

I'M ABOUT TO DIE...OVER A SOCCER MATCH!?

CHAPTER 2. ENTER THE ASSASSIN – END

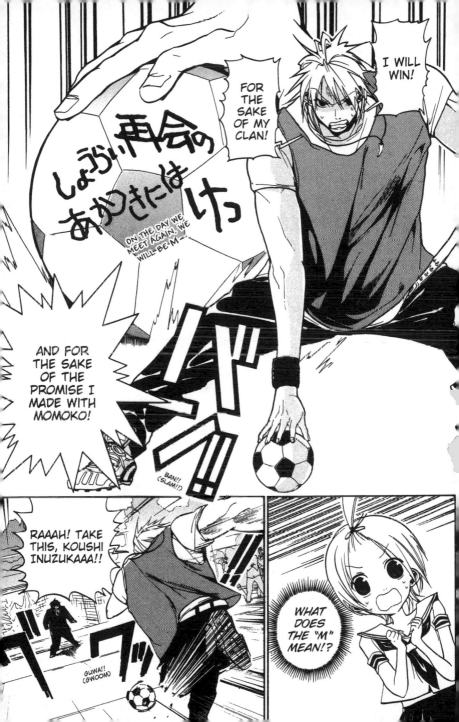

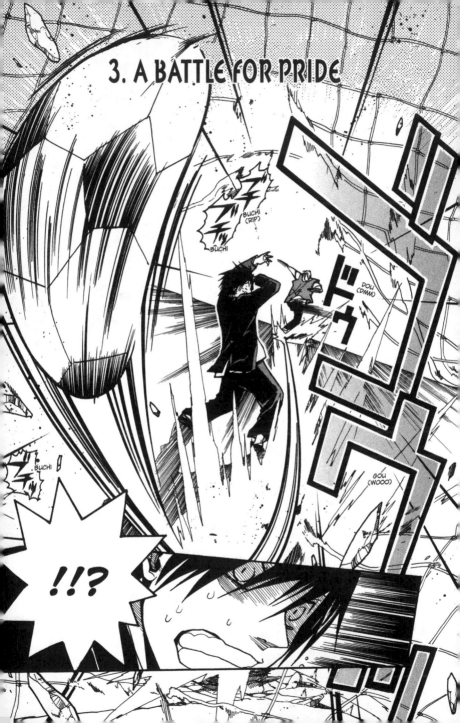

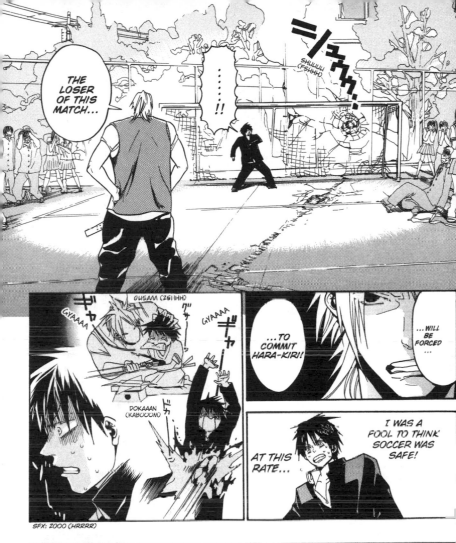

THE LOSER OF THIS MATCH...

!!

SHUUUU (FSHHH)

GYAAAA

GUSAM (ZGIIHH)

GYAAAA

DOKAAAN (KABOOOM)

...TO COMMIT HARA-KIRI!

...WILL BE FORCED...

AT THIS RATE...

I WAS A FOOL TO THINK SOCCER WAS SAFE!

SFX: ZOOO (HRRRR)

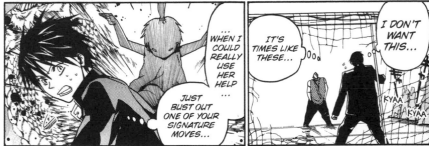

...WHEN I COULD REALLY USE HER HELP...

JUST BUST OUT ONE OF YOUR SIGNATURE MOVES...

IT'S TIMES LIKE THESE...

I DON'T WANT THIS...

KYAA

KYAA

123

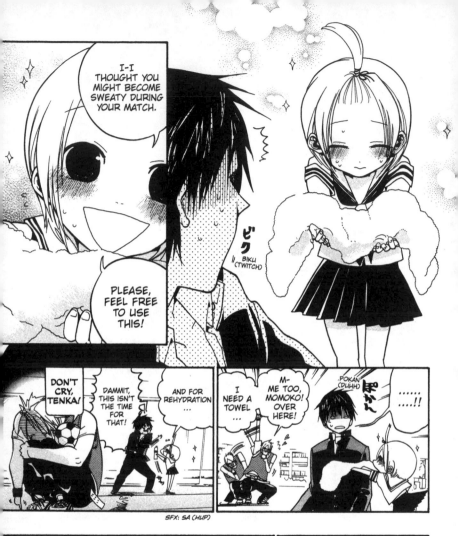

I-I THOUGHT YOU MIGHT BECOME SWEATY DURING YOUR MATCH.

ビク
BIKU (TWITCH)

PLEASE, FEEL FREE TO USE THIS!

DON'T CRY, TENKA!

DAMMIT, THIS ISN'T THE TIME FOR THAT!

AND FOR REHYDRATION...

I NEED A TOWEL...

M-ME TOO, MOMOKO! OVER HERE!

.POKAN (DUHH)
ぽかん

......
.....!!

SFX: SA (HUP)

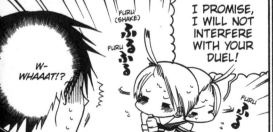

W-WHAAAT!?

FURU (SHAKE)
ふるふる
FURU

FURU
ふる

I PROMISE, I WILL NOT INTERFERE WITH YOUR DUEL!

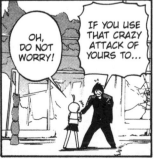

OH, DO NOT WORRY!

IF YOU USE THAT CRAZY ATTACK OF YOURS TO...

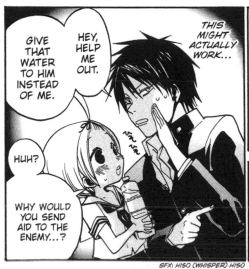

GIVE THAT WATER TO HIM INSTEAD OF ME.

HEY, HELP ME OUT.

THIS MIGHT ACTUALLY WORK...

HUH?

WHY WOULD YOU SEND AID TO THE ENEMY...?

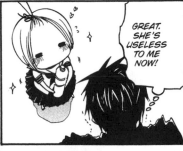

GREAT. SHE'S USELESS TO ME NOW!

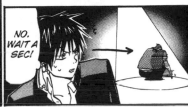

NO. WAIT A SEC!

SFX: HISO (WHISPER) HISO

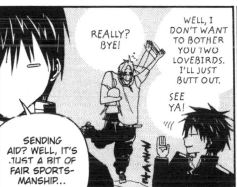

REALLY? BYE!

WELL, I DON'T WANT TO BOTHER YOU TWO LOVEBIRDS. I'LL JUST BUTT OUT.

SEE YA!

SENDING AID? WELL, IT'S JUST A BIT OF FAIR SPORTS-MANSHIP...

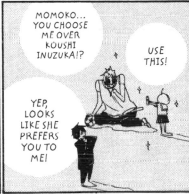

MOMOKO... YOU CHOOSE ME OVER KOUSHI INUZUKA!?

USE THIS!

YEP, LOOKS LIKE SHE PREFERS YOU TO ME!

SFX: SOSOKUSA (STEP STEP)

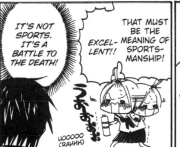

IT'S NOT SPORTS. IT'S A BATTLE TO THE DEATH!

THAT MUST BE THE MEANING OF SPORTS-MANSHIP!

EXCEL-LENT!!

UOOOOO (RAHHH)

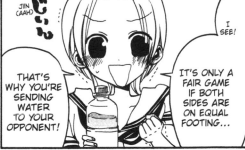

JIIN (AAH)

THAT'S WHY YOU'RE SENDING WATER TO YOUR OPPONENT!

I SEE!

IT'S ONLY A FAIR GAME IF BOTH SIDES ARE ON EQUAL FOOTING...

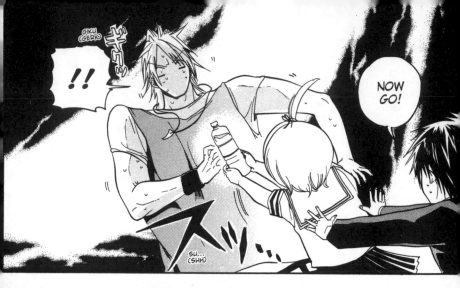

NOW GO!

GIKU (GERK)

!!

SU... (SHH)

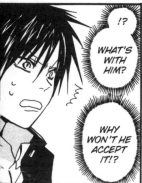

!?

WHAT'S WITH HIM?

WHY WON'T HE ACCEPT IT!?

I THINK I'LL PASS!

KI (KRK)

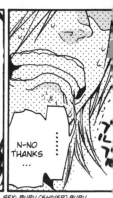

N-NO THANKS...

SFX: BURU (SHIVER) BURU

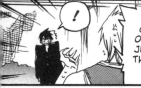

!

C-COME ON, LET'S JUST GET THIS OVER WITH!

MAYBE HE NOTICED MY HIDDEN INTENT!

HE'S ON ALERT.

FUUU (CHISSS)

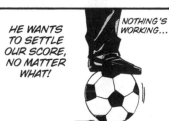

HE WANTS TO SETTLE OUR SCORE, NO MATTER WHAT!

NOTHING'S WORKING...

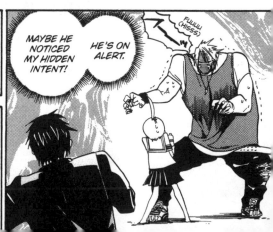

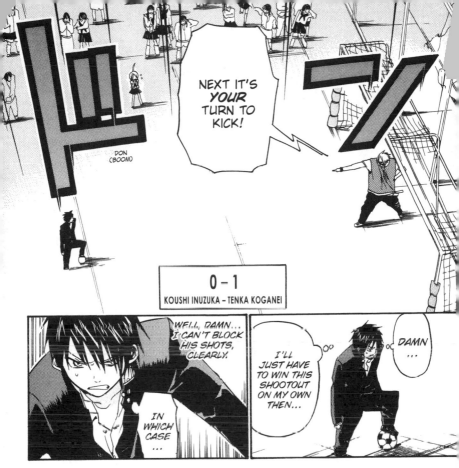

NEXT IT'S *YOUR* TURN TO KICK!

DON (BOOM)

0 - 1
KOUSHI INUZUKA – TENKA KOGANEI

WELL, DAMN... I CAN'T BLOCK HIS SHOTS, CLEARLY.

IN WHICH CASE...

I'LL JUST HAVE TO WIN THIS SHOOTOUT ON MY OWN THEN...

DAMN...

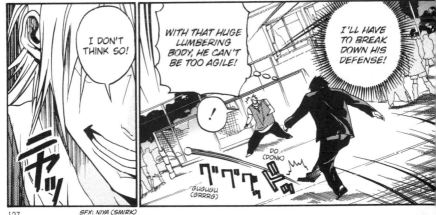

I DON'T THINK SO!

WITH THAT HUGE LUMBERING BODY, HE CAN'T BE TOO AGILE!

I'LL HAVE TO BREAK DOWN HIS DEFENSE!

DO (DONK)

GUGUGU (GRRRG)

SFX: NIYA (SMIRK)

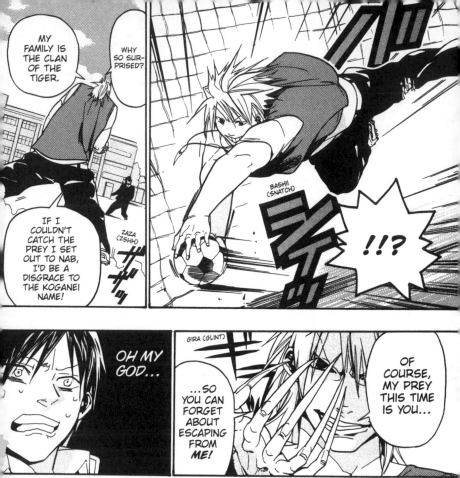

MY FAMILY IS THE CLAN OF THE TIGER.

WHY SO SURPRISED?

BASHII (SNATCH)

ZAZA (ZSHH)

IF I COULDN'T CATCH THE PREY I SET OUT TO NAB, I'D BE A DISGRACE TO THE KOGANEI NAME!

!!?

OH MY GOD...

GIRA (GLINT)

...SO YOU CAN FORGET ABOUT ESCAPING FROM ME!

OF COURSE, MY PREY THIS TIME IS YOU...

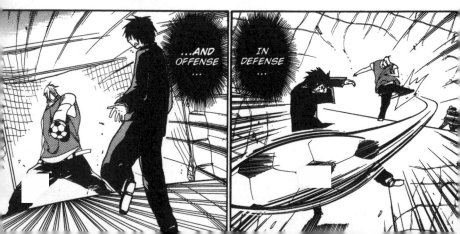

...AND OFFENSE...

IN DEFENSE...

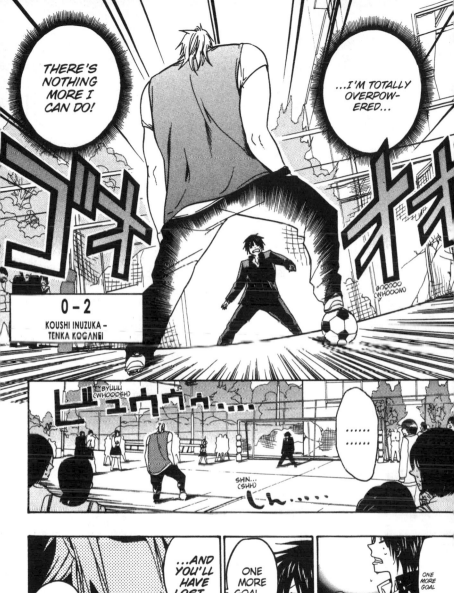

THERE'S NOTHING MORE I CAN DO!

...I'M TOTALLY OVERPOW-ERED...

0 - 2
KOUSHI INUZUKA -
TENKA KOGANEI

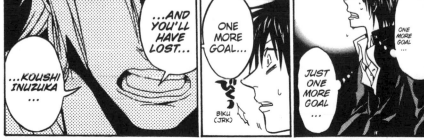

...AND YOU'LL HAVE LOST...

...KOUSHI INUZUKA...

ONE MORE GOAL...

ONE MORE GOAL...

JUST ONE MORE GOAL...

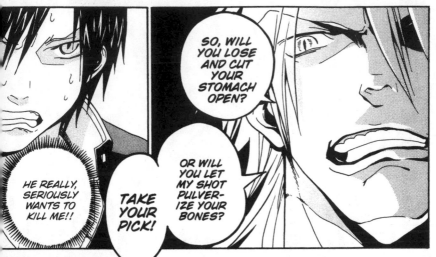

SO, WILL YOU LOSE AND CUT YOUR STOMACH OPEN?

HE REALLY, SERIOUSLY WANTS TO KILL ME!!

TAKE YOUR PICK!

OR WILL YOU LET MY SHOT PULVERIZE YOUR BONES?

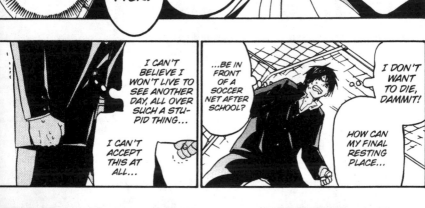

I CAN'T BELIEVE I WON'T LIVE TO SEE ANOTHER DAY, ALL OVER SUCH A STUPID THING...

I CAN'T ACCEPT THIS AT ALL...

...BE IN FRONT OF A SOCCER NET AFTER SCHOOL?

I DON'T WANT TO DIE, DAMMIT!

HOW CAN MY FINAL RESTING PLACE...

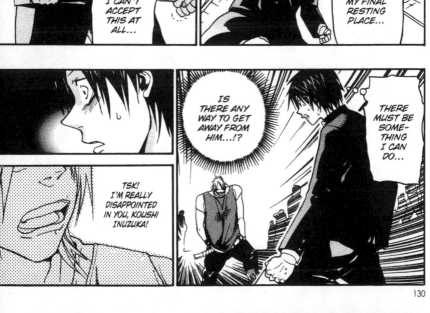

IS THERE ANY WAY TO GET AWAY FROM HIM...!?

THERE MUST BE SOMETHING I CAN DO...

TSK! I'M REALLY DISAPPOINTED IN YOU, KOUSHI INUZUKA!

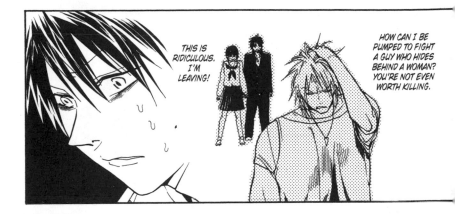

THIS IS RIDICULOUS. I'M LEAVING!

HOW CAN I BE PUMPED TO FIGHT A GUY WHO HIDES BEHIND A WOMAN? YOU'RE NOT EVEN WORTH KILLING.

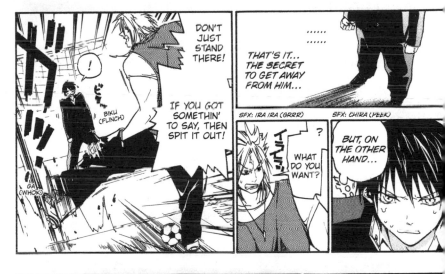

DON'T JUST STAND THERE!

IF YOU GOT SOMETHIN' TO SAY, THEN SPIT IT OUT!

BIKU (FLINCH)

GA! (WHOK)

......
......

THAT'S IT... THE SECRET TO GET AWAY FROM HIM...

SFX: IRA IRA (GRRR)

SFX: CHIRA (PEEK)

?

WHAT DO YOU WANT?

BUT, ON THE OTHER HAND...

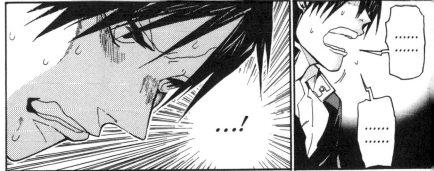

...!

......
......

......
......

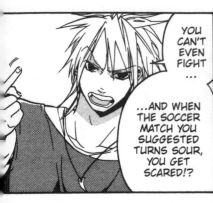

YOU CAN'T EVEN FIGHT...

...AND WHEN THE SOCCER MATCH YOU SUGGESTED TURNS SOUR, YOU GET SCARED!?

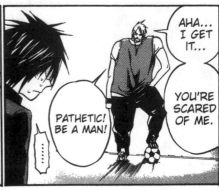

AHA... I GET IT...

PATHETIC! BE A MAN!

YOU'RE SCARED OF ME.

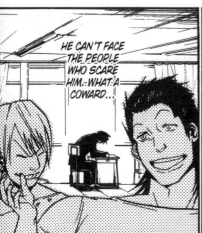

HE CAN'T FACE THE PEOPLE WHO SCARE HIM. WHAT A COWARD...

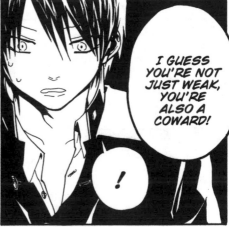

I GUESS YOU'RE NOT JUST WEAK, YOU'RE ALSO A COWARD!

!

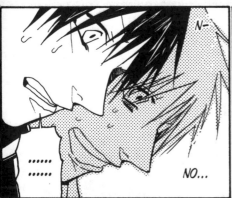

N—

......
......

NO...

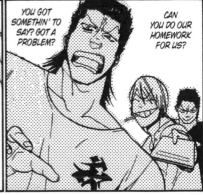

YOU GOT SOMETHIN' TO SAY? GOT A PROBLEM?

CAN YOU DO OUR HOMEWORK FOR US?

I FELT THE SAME WAY WHEN I WAS A SLAVE TO THOSE THUGS...

DAMMIT... I KNOW THIS FEELING...

COMPARED TO A POWERFUL AND BRAVE GUY LIKE ME, OF COURSE!

SIGH!

MAN, KOUSHI INUZUKA IS ONE PATHETIC WIMP!

!

KOUSHI-DONO...?

ZAWA (MURMUR)

ZAWA

M-MOMOKO...

KOUSHI-DONO IS NOTHING LIKE THAT!

HE DOESN'T HAVE THE LEAST SHRED OF MANLI—

HE'S AFRAID OF MY STRENGTH AND COURAGE!

......
......

HEY! KOUSHI INUZUKA!

ZUI (ZUMM)

SEE?

YOU'RE WRONG!

LOOK AT HIM! HE'S GOT NO GUTS!

O-

OPEN YOUR EYES!

COLD SWEAT, A PAINFUL LUMP AT THE BACK OF MY THROAT. ONCE I GET THIS WAY...

I KNOW THIS FEELING, BECAUSE I'VE EXPERIENCED IT MANY TIMES BEFORE.

ARE YOU GONNA OBEY MY COMMANDS...

...OR AREN'T YOU...?

SFX: GIRO (GLARE)

SFX: GUI (TUG)

BORO (BLONK)

THERE'S NOTHING ELSE I CAN DO, I GUESS...

...BY MEN STRONGER THAN ME...

WHENEVER I GET THREATENED...

...I HAVE NO CHOICE BUT TO OBEY THEM...

DARAN (SLUMP)

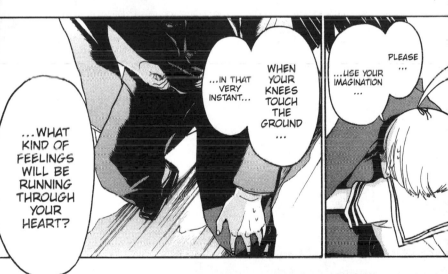

...WHAT
KIND OF
FEELINGS
WILL BE
RUNNING
THROUGH
YOUR
HEART?

...IN THAT
VERY
INSTANT...

WHEN
YOUR
KNEES
TOUCH
THE
GROUND
...

...USE YOUR
IMAGINATION
...

PLEASE
...

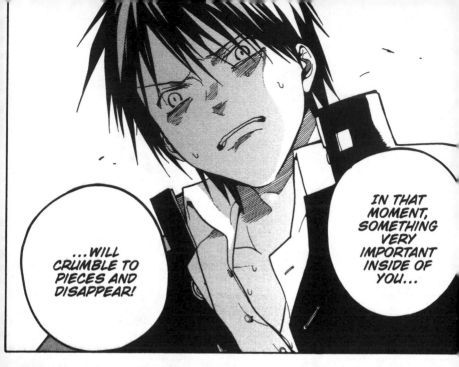

...WILL CRUMBLE TO PIECES AND DISAPPEAR!

IN THAT MOMENT, SOMETHING VERY IMPORTANT INSIDE OF YOU...

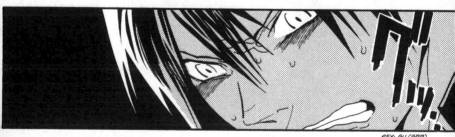

SFX: GU (GRR)

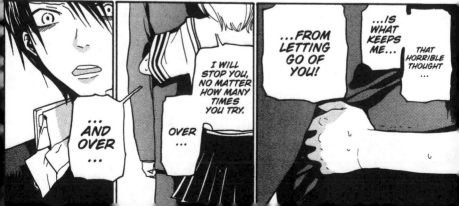

I WILL STOP YOU, NO MATTER HOW MANY TIMES YOU TRY.

...FROM LETTING GO OF YOU!

...IS WHAT KEEPS ME...

THAT HORRIBLE THOUGHT...

...AND OVER...

OVER...

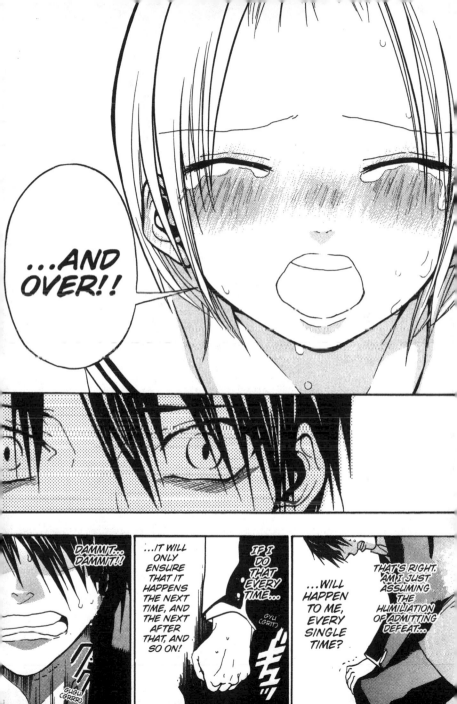

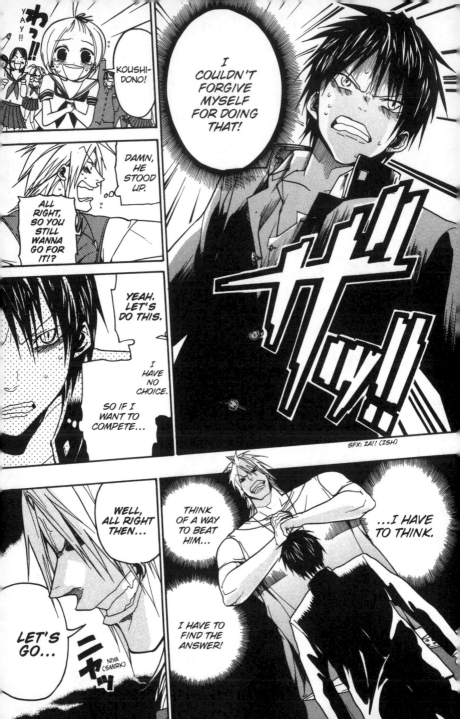

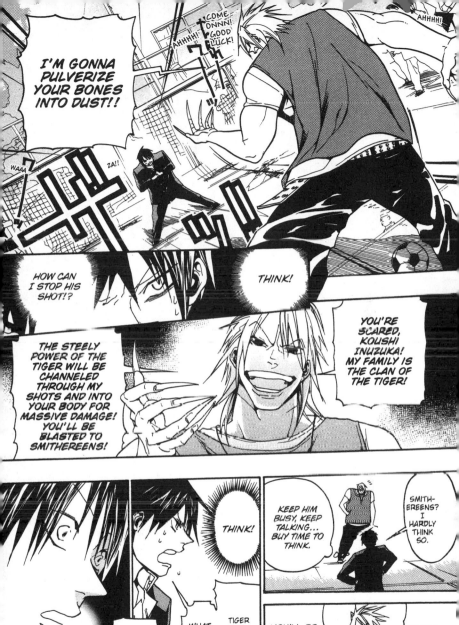

FUUU
(MISS)

AND THAT'S WHY HE...

V W
OOOAAAAAAA
(WAAAAHH)

STAY MY PARTNER FOREVER, WON'T-CHA!?

AWW, THANKS, BECKY! YOU'RE THE BEST CHICK A GUY COULD EVER KNOW!

WE CAN NEVER FULFILL OUR PROMISE, NOW...

!!

OF COURSE...

MOMOKO'S FORGOTTE ALL ABOU ME.

SFX: GORO (PURR)

SFX: KARI (SCRATCH) KARI KARI KARI KARI KARI!

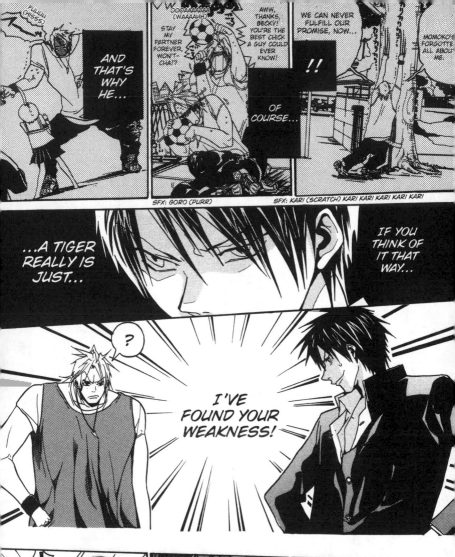

...A TIGER REALLY IS JUST...

IF YOU THINK OF IT THAT WAY...

?

I'VE FOUND YOUR WEAKNESS!

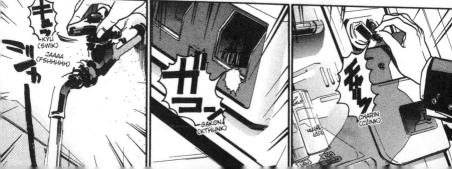

ギュ
KYU (SWIK)

ジャアア
JAAAA (FSHHHHH)

ガコン
GAKON (KTHUNK)

チャリン
CHARIN (CLIINK)

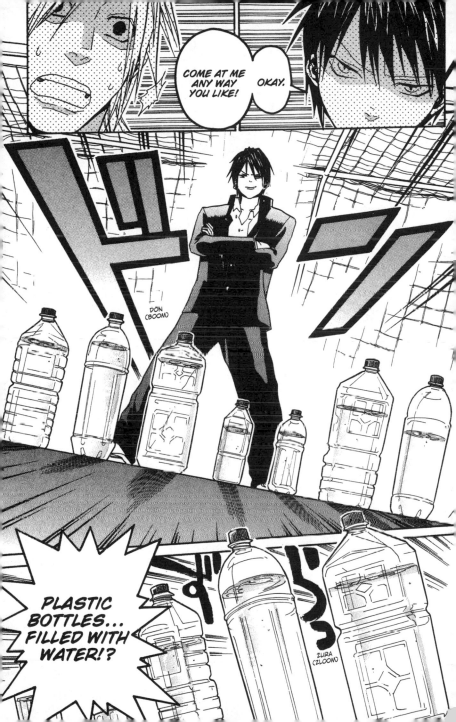

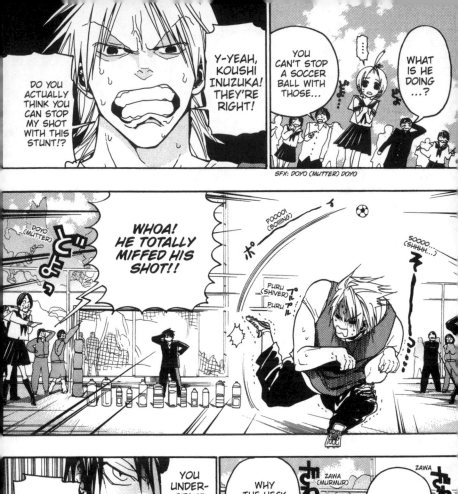
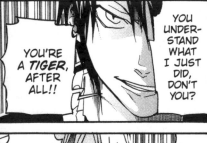
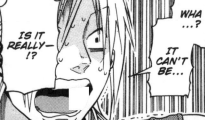
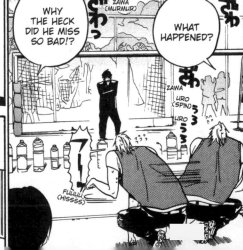

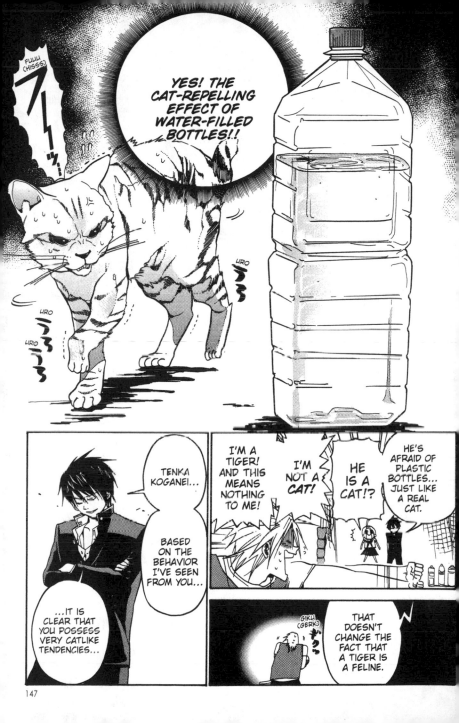

FUUU (CHISS!)

YES! THE CAT-REPELLING EFFECT OF WATER-FILLED BOTTLES!!

URO

URO

URO

TENKA KOGANEI...

BASED ON THE BEHAVIOR I'VE SEEN FROM YOU...

...IT IS CLEAR THAT YOU POSSESS VERY CATLIKE TENDENCIES...

I'M A TIGER! AND THIS MEANS NOTHING TO ME!

I'M NOT A CAT!

HE IS A CAT!?

HE'S AFRAID OF PLASTIC BOTTLES... JUST LIKE A REAL CAT.

GIKU (GERK)

THAT DOESN'T CHANGE THE FACT THAT A TIGER IS A FELINE.

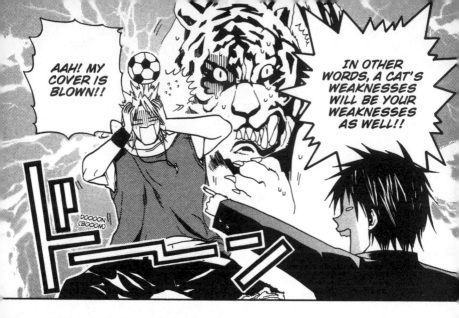

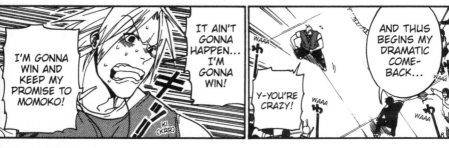

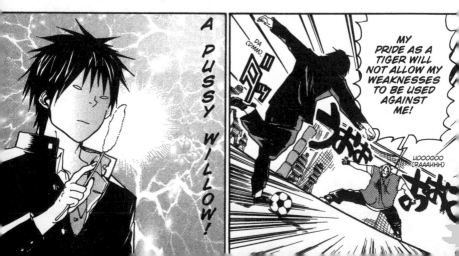

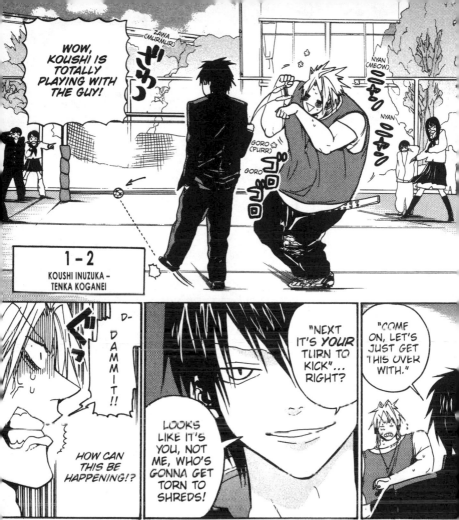

WOW, KOUSHI IS TOTALLY PLAYING WITH THE GUY!

ZAWA (MURMUR)

NYAN (MEOW)

NYAN

GORO (PURR)

GORO

1 - 2
KOUSHI INUZUKA - TENKA KOGANEI

D-DAMMIT!!

HOW CAN THIS BE HAPPENING!?

LOOKS LIKE IT'S YOU, NOT ME, WHO'S GONNA GET TORN TO SHREDS!

"NEXT IT'S *YOUR* TURN TO KICK"... RIGHT?

"COME ON, LET'S JUST GET THIS OVER WITH."

GFX: GU (GRR)

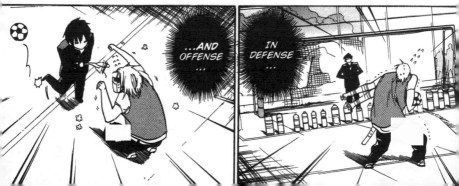

...AND OFFENSE...

IN DEFENSE...

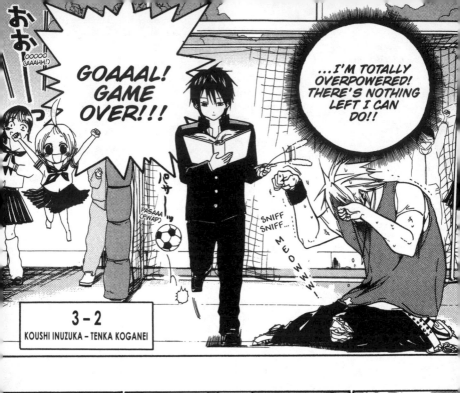

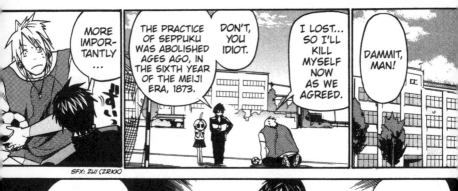

SFX: ZUI (ZRKK)

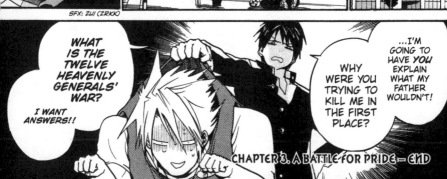

CHAPTER 3. A BATTLE FOR PRIDE — END

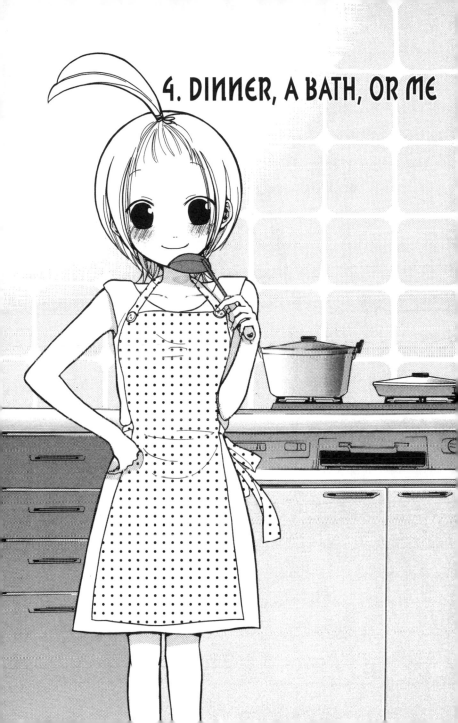

4. DINNER, A BATH, OR ME

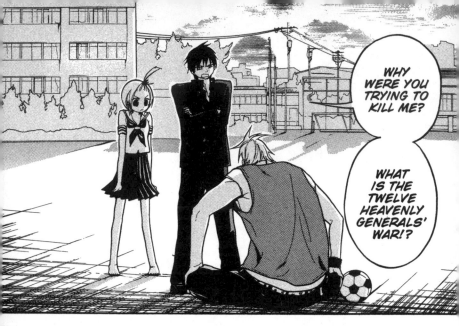

WHY WERE YOU TRYING TO KILL ME?

WHAT IS THE TWELVE HEAVENLY GENERALS' WAR!?

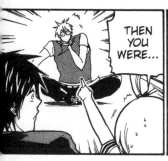

THEN YOU WERE...

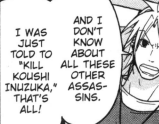

I WAS JUST TOLD TO "KILL KOUSHI INUZUKA," THAT'S ALL!

AND I DON'T KNOW ABOUT ALL THESE OTHER ASSAS- SINS.

I-I DON'T KNOW! I DON'T KNOW ALL THE COMPLICATED DETAILS!

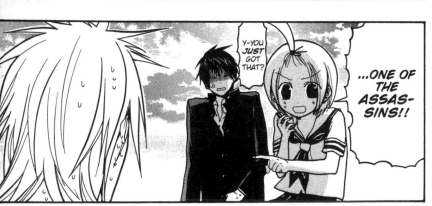

Y-YOU JUST GOT THAT?

...ONE OF THE ASSAS- SINS!!

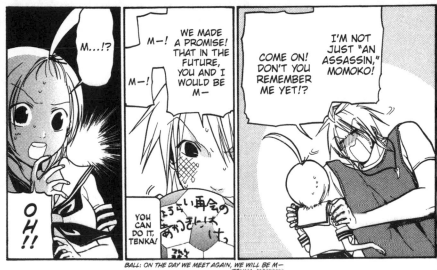

M...!?

M—!

M—!

WE MADE A PROMISE! THAT IN THE FUTURE, YOU AND I WOULD BE M—

COME ON! DON'T YOU REMEMBER ME YET!?

I'M NOT JUST "AN ASSASSIN," MOMOKO!

OH!!

YOU CAN DO IT, TENKA!

BALL: ON THE DAY WE MEET AGAIN, WE WILL BE M—
TENKA, MOMOKO

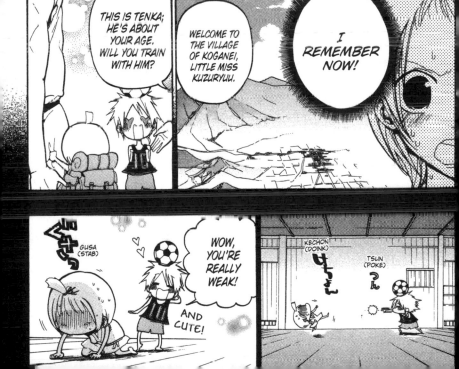

THIS IS TENKA; HE'S ABOUT YOUR AGE. WILL YOU TRAIN WITH HIM?

WELCOME TO THE VILLAGE OF KOGANEI, LITTLE MISS KUZURYUU.

I REMEMBER NOW!

GUSA (STAB)

WOW, YOU'RE REALLY WEAK!

AND CUTE!

KECHON (DOINK)

TSUN (POKE)

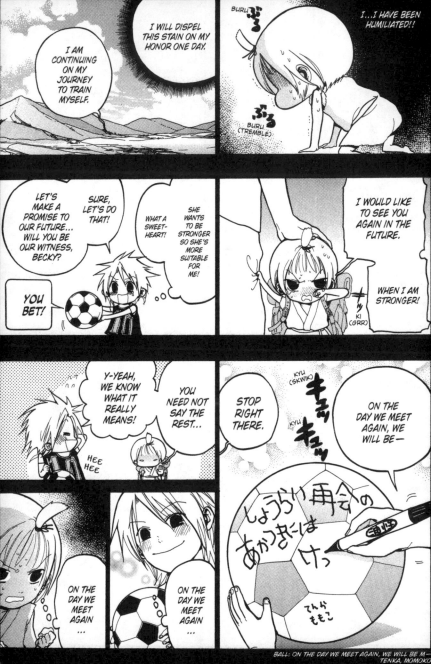

BALL: ON THE DAY WE MEET AGAIN, WE WILL BE M—, TENKA, MOMOKO

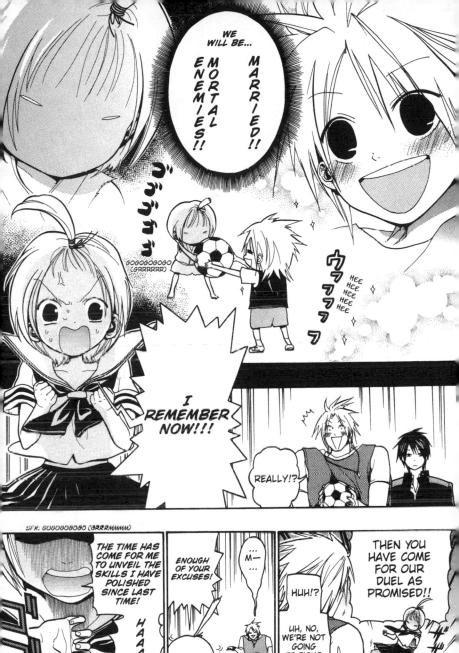
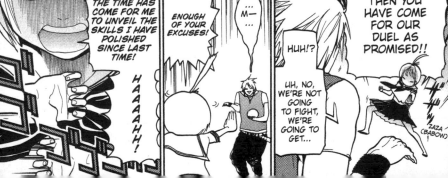

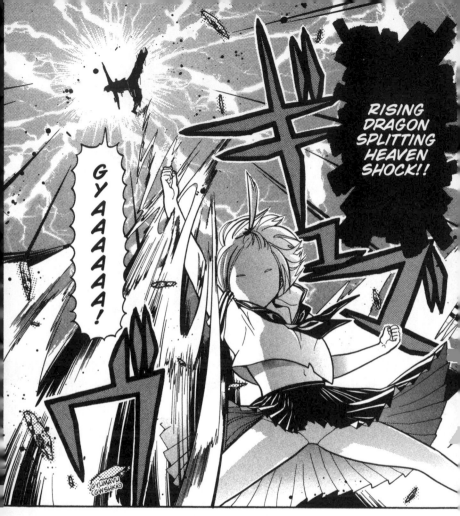

RISING DRAGON SPLITTING HEAVEN SHOCK!!

GYAAAAA!

GYUMMMU! (CWSHKO)

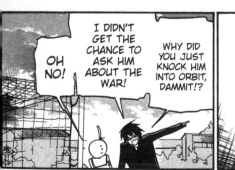

OH NO!

I DIDN'T GET THE CHANCE TO ASK HIM ABOUT THE WAR!

WHY DID YOU JUST KNOCK HIM INTO ORBIT, DAMMIT!?

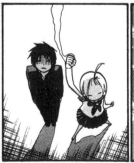

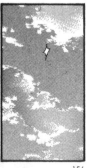

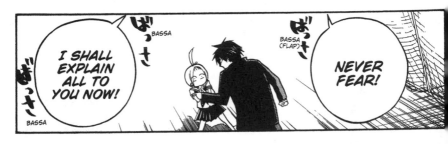

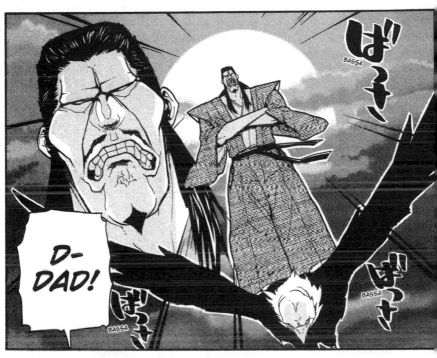

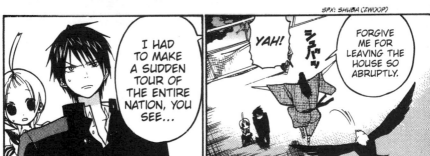

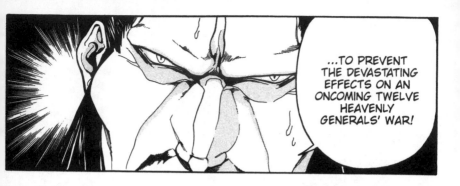

...TO PREVENT THE DEVASTATING EFFECTS ON AN ONCOMING TWELVE HEAVENLY GENERALS' WAR!

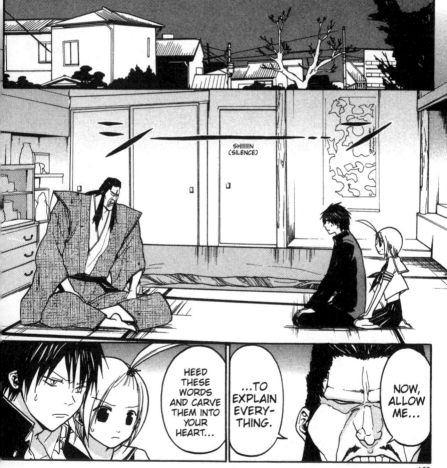

SHIIIIIN
(SILENCE)

HEED THESE WORDS AND CARVE THEM INTO YOUR HEART...

...TO EXPLAIN EVERY-THING.

NOW, ALLOW ME...

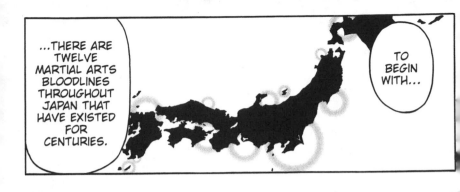

...THERE ARE TWELVE MARTIAL ARTS BLOODLINES THROUGHOUT JAPAN THAT HAVE EXISTED FOR CENTURIES.

TO BEGIN WITH...

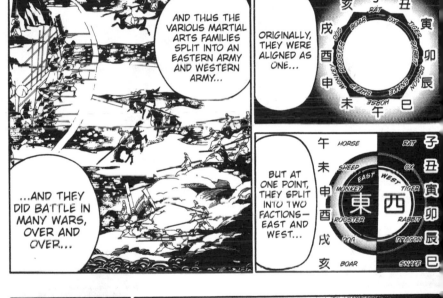

AND THUS THE VARIOUS MARTIAL ARTS FAMILIES SPLIT INTO AN EASTERN ARMY AND WESTERN ARMY...

...AND THEY DID BATTLE IN MANY WARS, OVER AND OVER...

ORIGINALLY, THEY WERE ALIGNED AS ONE...

亥 子 丑
戌 寅
酉 卯
申 辰
未 午
RAT OX TIGER RABBIT DRAGON SNAKE HORSE SHEEP MONKEY ROOSTER DOG BOAR

BUT AT ONE POINT, THEY SPLIT INTO TWO FACTIONS— EAST AND WEST...

午 HORSE
未 SHEEP
申 MONKEY
酉 ROOSTER
戌
亥 BOAR
東 EAST
西 WEST
子 RAT
丑 OX
寅 TIGER
卯 RABBIT
辰 DRAGON
巳 SNAKE

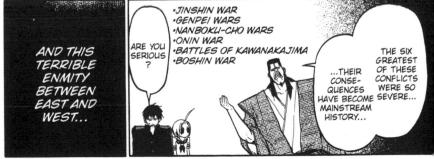

AND THIS TERRIBLE ENMITY BETWEEN EAST AND WEST...

ARE YOU SERIOUS?

•JINSHIN WAR
•GENPEI WARS
•NANBOKU-CHO WARS
•ONIN WAR
•BATTLES OF KAWANAKAJIMA
•BOSHIN WAR

...THEIR CONSE-QUENCES HAVE BECOME MAINSTREAM HISTORY...

THE SIX GREATEST OF THESE CONFLICTS WERE SO SEVERE...

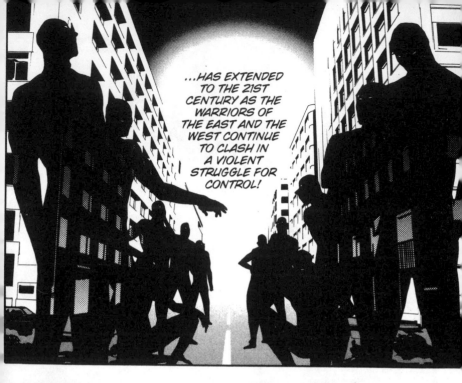

...HAS EXTENDED TO THE 21ST CENTURY AS THE WARRIORS OF THE EAST AND THE WEST CONTINUE TO CLASH IN A VIOLENT STRUGGLE FOR CONTROL!

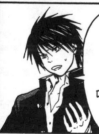

IS IT REALLY ALL *THAT* DANGEROUS?

SO YOU'RE SAYING... THESE MARTIAL ARTS FAMILIES ARE HAVING A NATIONWIDE DISPUTE...?

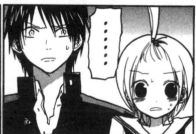

THE TOTAL POPULATION OF ALL THE MARTIAL ARTS CLANS NOW SPANS HUNDREDS OF THOUSANDS!

THE BLOOD OF THE TWELVE HEAVENLY GENERALS HAS SPREAD WIDE THROUGH THE GENERAL POPULACE OVER TIME.

DO NOT LOOK UPON THESE EVENTS LIGHTLY, BOY!

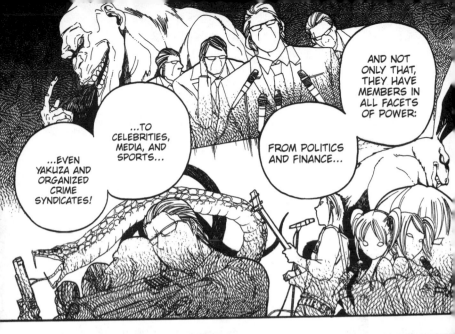

AND NOT ONLY THAT, THEY HAVE MEMBERS IN ALL FACETS OF POWER:

FROM POLITICS AND FINANCE...

...TO CELEBRITIES, MEDIA, AND SPORTS...

...EVEN YAKUZA AND ORGANIZED CRIME SYNDICATES!

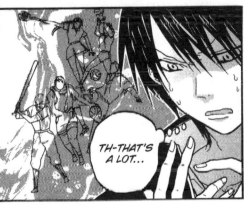

FOR EXAMPLE, THINK OF ALL THE SPORTS PLAYERS YOU CAN IMAGINE, WITH "TORA" (TIGER) IN THEIR LAST NAME.

TH-THAT'S A LOT...

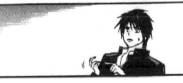

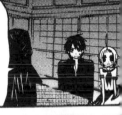

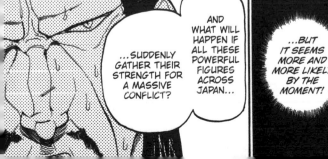

...SUDDENLY GATHER THEIR STRENGTH FOR A MASSIVE CONFLICT?

AND WHAT WILL HAPPEN IF ALL THESE POWERFUL FIGURES ACROSS JAPAN...

...BUT IT SEEMS MORE AND MORE LIKELY BY THE MOMENT!

THIS STRUCK ME AS A BUNCH OF CRAZY HOGWASH AT FIRST...

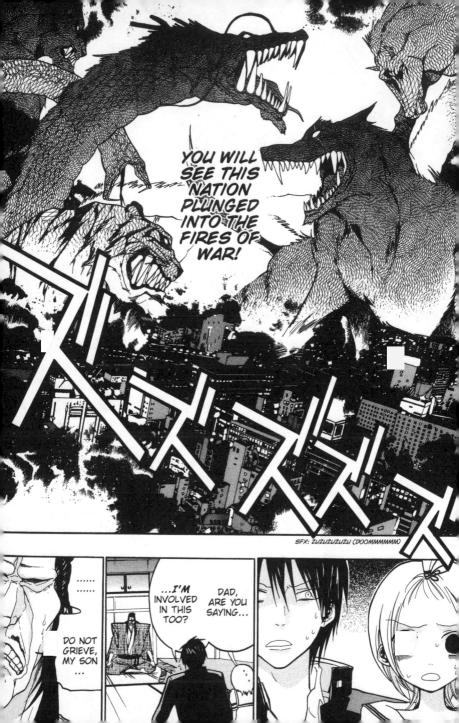

YOU WILL SEE THIS NATION PLUNGED INTO THE FIRES OF WAR!

SFX: ZUZUZUZUZU (DOOMMMMMMM)

......
......

DO NOT GRIEVE, MY SON ...

...I'M INVOLVED IN THIS TOO?

DAD, ARE YOU SAYING...

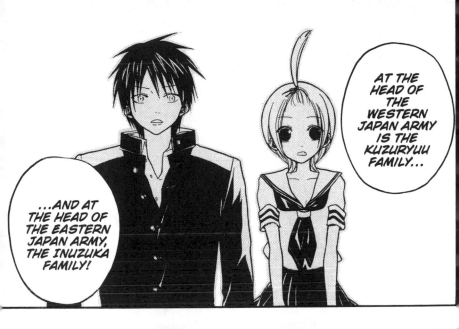

AT THE HEAD OF THE WESTERN JAPAN ARMY IS THE KUZURYUU FAMILY...

...AND AT THE HEAD OF THE EASTERN JAPAN ARMY, THE INUZUKA FAMILY!

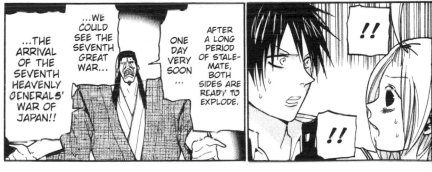

...THE ARRIVAL OF THE SEVENTH HEAVENLY GENERALS' WAR OF JAPAN!!

...WE COULD SEE THE SEVENTH GREAT WAR...

ONE DAY VERY SOON...

AFTER A LONG PERIOD OF STALE-MATE, BOTH SIDES ARE READY TO EXPLODE.

!!

!!

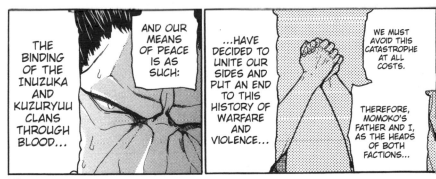

THE BINDING OF THE INUZUKA AND KUZURYUU CLANS THROUGH BLOOD...

AND OUR MEANS OF PEACE IS AS SUCH:

...HAVE DECIDED TO UNITE OUR SIDES AND PUT AN END TO THIS HISTORY OF WARFARE AND VIOLENCE...

WE MUST AVOID THIS CATASTROPHE AT ALL COSTS.

THEREFORE, MOMOKO'S FATHER AND I, AS THE HEADS OF BOTH FACTIONS...

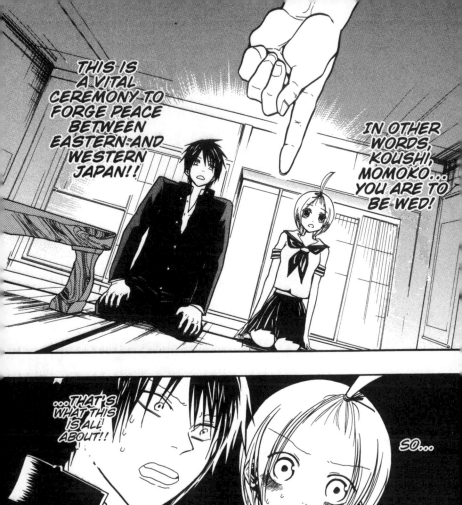

THIS IS A VITAL CEREMONY TO FORGE PEACE BETWEEN EASTERN AND WESTERN JAPAN!!

IN OTHER WORDS, KOUSHI, MOMOKO... YOU ARE TO BE WED!

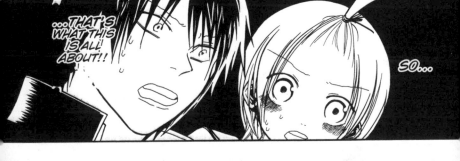

...THAT'S WHAT THIS IS ALL ABOUT!!

SO...

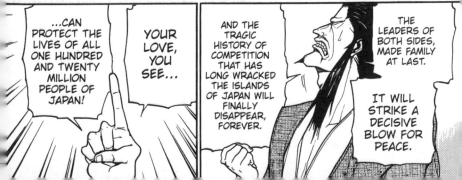

...CAN PROTECT THE LIVES OF ALL ONE HUNDRED AND TWENTY MILLION PEOPLE OF JAPAN!

YOUR LOVE, YOU SEE...

AND THE TRAGIC HISTORY OF COMPETITION THAT HAS LONG WRACKED THE ISLANDS OF JAPAN WILL FINALLY DISAPPEAR, FOREVER.

THE LEADERS OF BOTH SIDES, MADE FAMILY AT LAST.

IT WILL STRIKE A DECISIVE BLOW FOR PEACE.

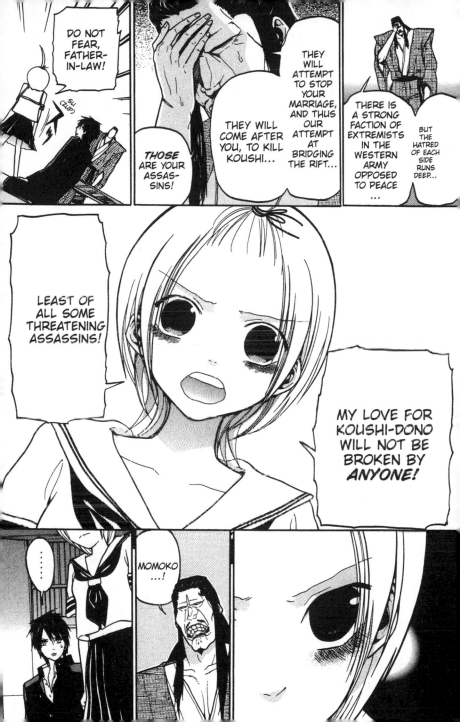

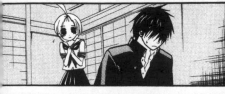

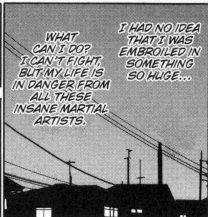

I HAD NO IDEA THAT I WAS EMBROILED IN SOMETHING SO HUGE...

WHAT CAN I DO? I CAN'T FIGHT, BUT MY LIFE IS IN DANGER FROM ALL THESE INSANE MARTIAL ARTISTS.

KOUSHI-DONO?

PLEASE DON'T LOOK THAT WAY...

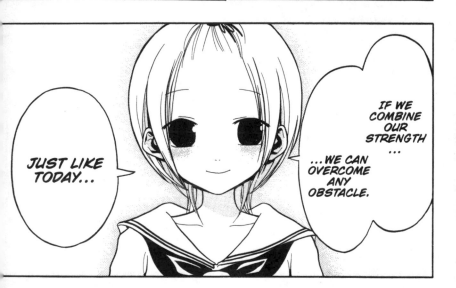

JUST LIKE TODAY...

IF WE COMBINE OUR STRENGTH...

...WE CAN OVERCOME ANY OBSTACLE.

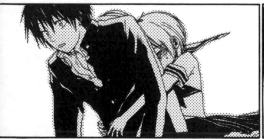

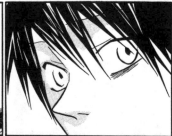

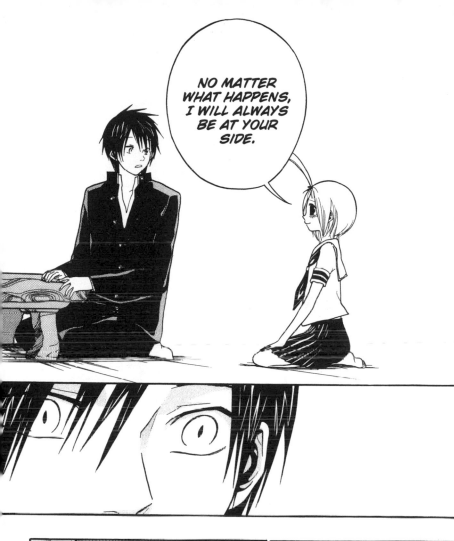

NO MATTER WHAT HAPPENS, I WILL ALWAYS BE AT YOUR SIDE.

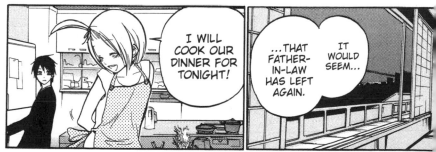

I WILL COOK OUR DINNER FOR TONIGHT!

...THAT FATHER-IN-LAW HAS LEFT AGAIN.

IT WOULD SEEM...

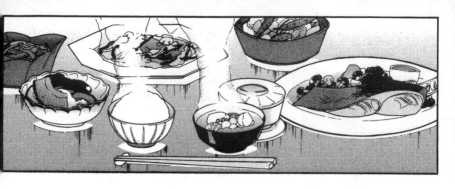

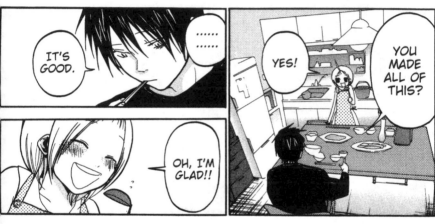

IT'S GOOD.

......
......

YES!

YOU MADE ALL OF THIS?

OH, I'M GLAD!!

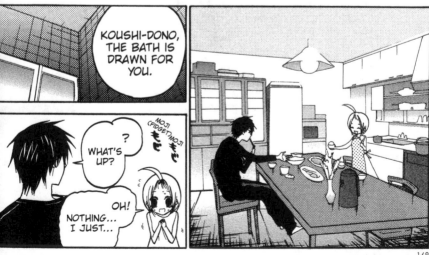

KOUSHI-DONO, THE BATH IS DRAWN FOR YOU.

WHAT'S UP?

?

MOJI
(FIDGET)
もじ もじ

OH! NOTHING... I JUST...

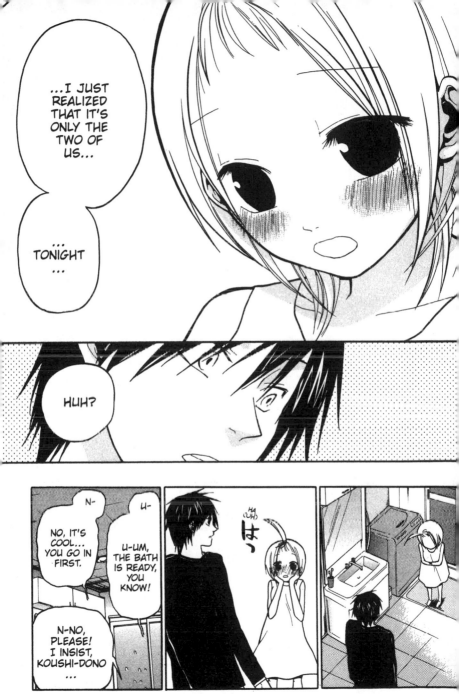

footer: 169

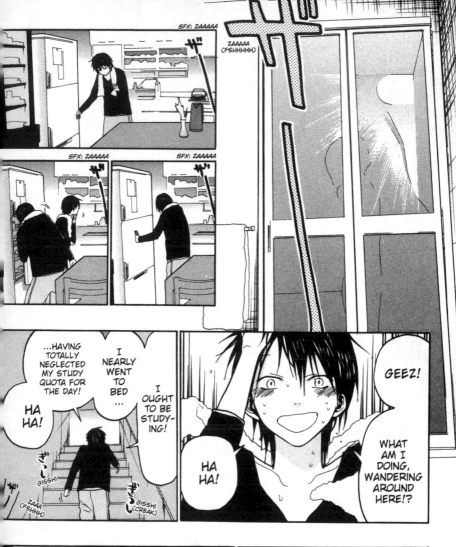

SFX: ZAAAAA

ZAAAAA
(FSHHHHH)

SFX: ZAAAAA

SFX: ZAAAAA

...HAVING TOTALLY NEGLECTED MY STUDY QUOTA FOR THE DAY!

I NEARLY WENT TO BED...

I OUGHT TO BE STUDY-ING!

HA HA!

HA HA!

GISSHI

ZAAA
(FSHHHD)

GISSHI
(CREAK)

GEEZ!

WHAT AM I DOING, WANDERING AROUND HERE!?

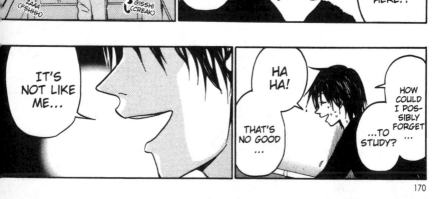

IT'S NOT LIKE ME...

HA HA!

THAT'S NO GOOD...

HOW COULD I POS-SIBLY FORGET...

...TO STUDY?

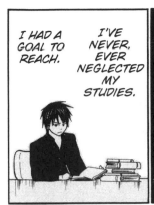

I HAD A GOAL TO REACH.

I'VE NEVER, EVER NEGLECTED MY STUDIES.

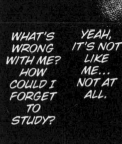

WHAT'S WRONG WITH ME? HOW COULD I FORGET TO STUDY?

YEAH, IT'S NOT LIKE ME... NOT AT ALL.

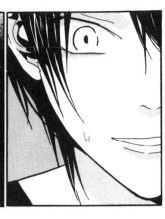

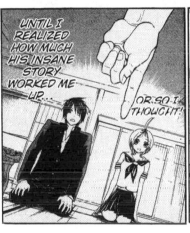

UNTIL I REALIZED HOW MUCH HIS INSANE STORY WORKED ME UP...

OR, SO I THOUGHT!

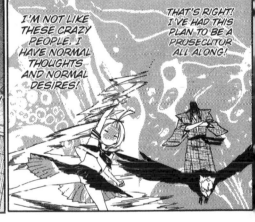

I'M NOT LIKE THESE CRAZY PEOPLE. I HAVE NORMAL THOUGHTS AND NORMAL DESIRES!

THAT'S RIGHT! I'VE HAD THIS PLAN TO BE A PROSECUTOR ALL ALONG!

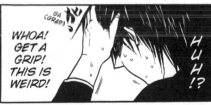

GA (GRAB)

WHOA! GET A GRIP! THIS IS WEIRD!

HUH!?

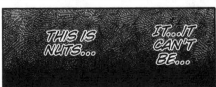

THIS IS NUTS...

IT...IT CAN'T BE...

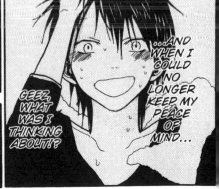

GEEZ, WHAT WAS I THINKING ABOUT!?

...AND WHEN I COULD NO LONGER KEEP MY PEACE OF MIND...

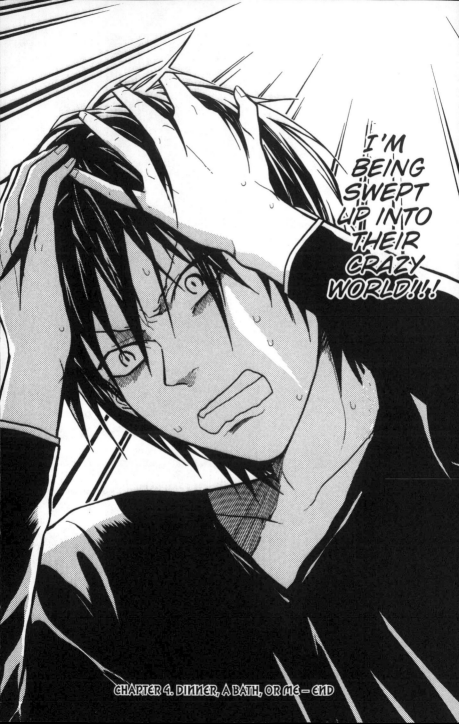

I'M BEING BEING SWEPT UP INTO THEIR CRAZY WORLD!!!

CHAPTER 4. DINNER, A BATH, OR ME — END

5. INVISIBLE BONDS

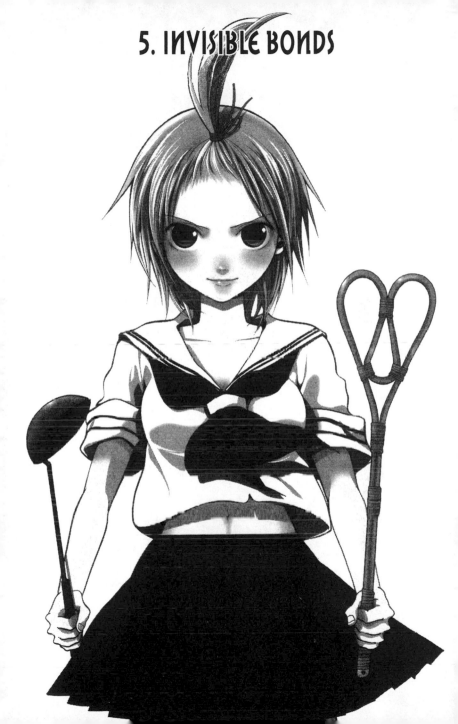

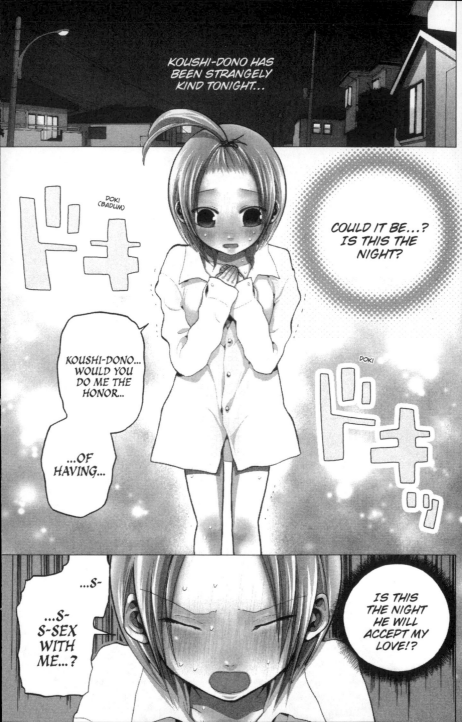

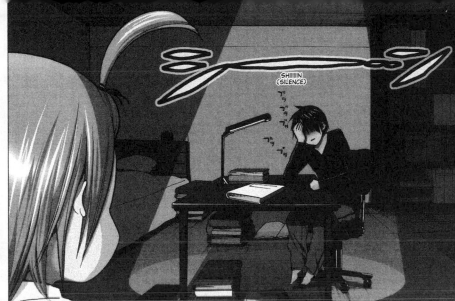

SHIIIIIN
(SILENCE)

SFX: BUTSU (MUTTER) BUTSU BUTSU BUTSU BUTSU

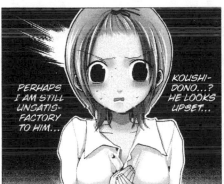

PERHAPS I AM STILL UNSATISFACTORY TO HIM...

KOUSHI-DONO...? HE LOOKS UPSET...

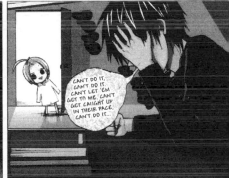

CAN'T DO IT, CAN'T DO IT, CAN'T LET 'EM GET TO ME, CAN'T GET CAUGHT UP IN THEIR PACE, CAN'T DO IT...

SFX: BUTSU BUTSU BUTSU BUTSU BUTSU

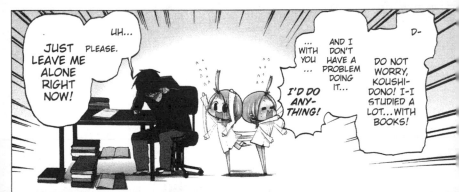

JUST LEAVE ME ALONE RIGHT NOW!

UH... PLEASE.

... WITH YOU ...

AND I DON'T HAVE A PROBLEM DOING IT...

I'D DO ANYTHING!

D-

DO NOT WORRY, KOUSHI-DONO! I-I STUDIED A LOT...WITH BOOKS!

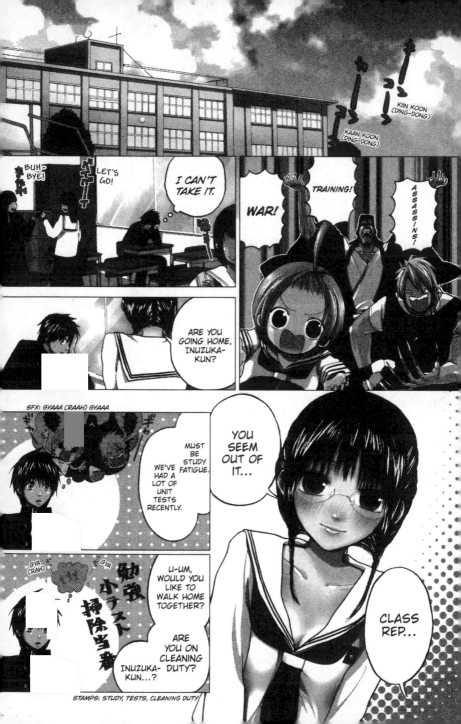

KIIN KOON
(DING-DONG)

KAAN KOON
(DING-DONG)

BUH-BYE!

LET'S GO!

I CAN'T TAKE IT.

WAR!

TRAINING!

ASSASSINS!

ARE YOU GOING HOME, INUZUKA-KUN?

SFX: GYAAA (RAAH) GYAAA

MUST BE STUDY FATIGUE.

WE'VE HAD A LOT OF UNIT TESTS RECENTLY.

YOU SEEM OUT OF IT...

GYA (RAAH)

GYA

U-UM, WOULD YOU LIKE TO WALK HOME TOGETHER?

ARE YOU ON CLEANING DUTY INUZUKA-KUN...?

CLASS REP...

STAMPS: STUDY, TESTS, CLEANING DUTY

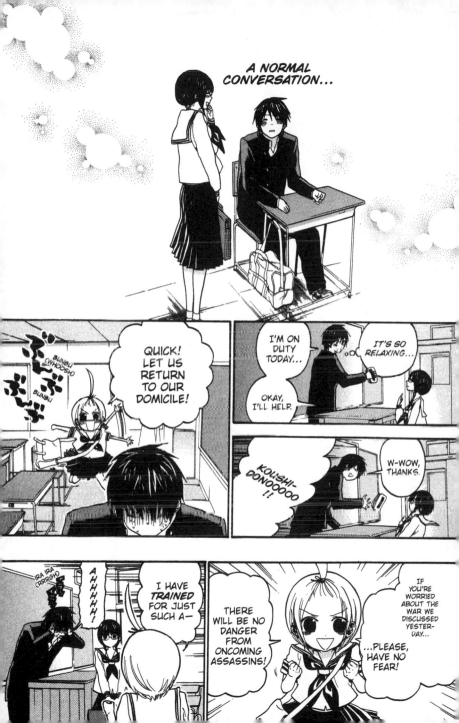

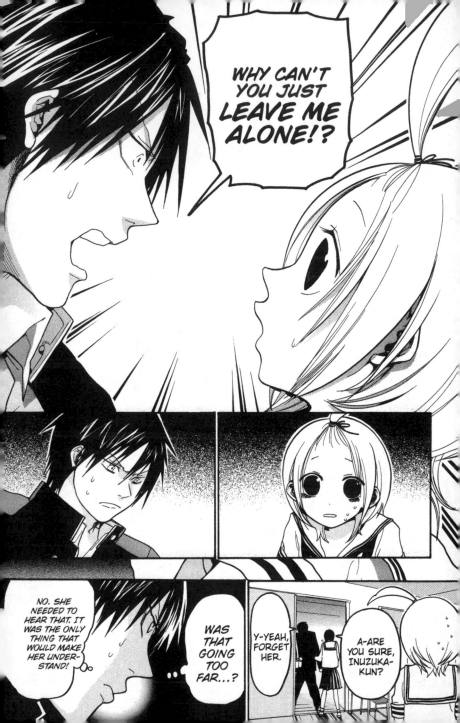

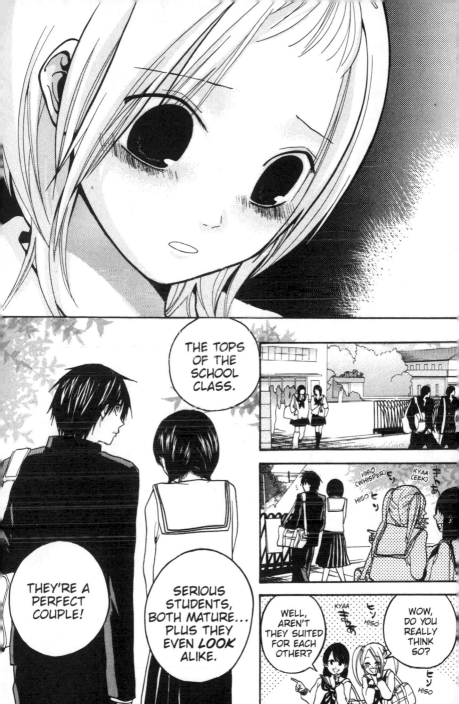

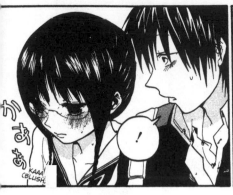
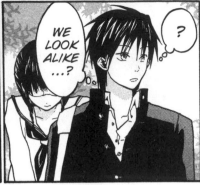

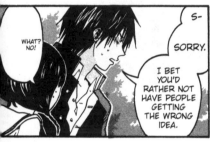
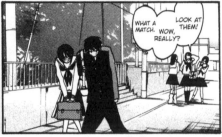

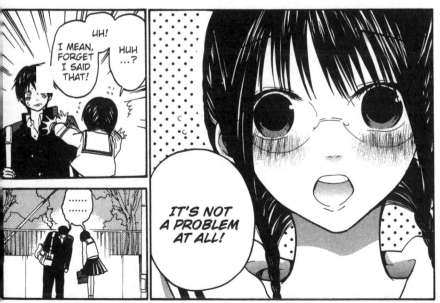

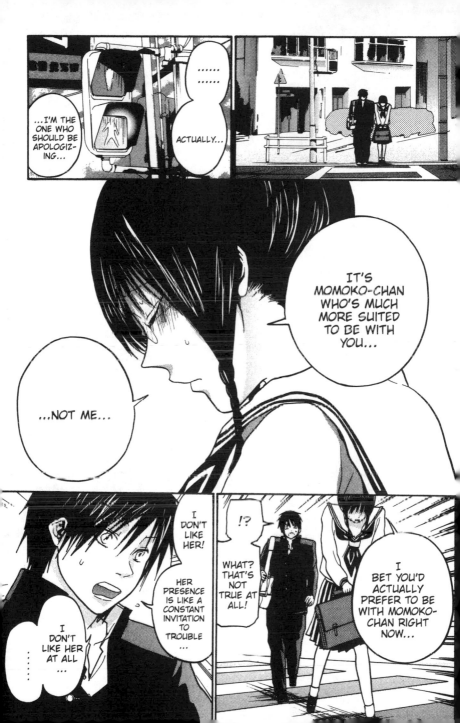

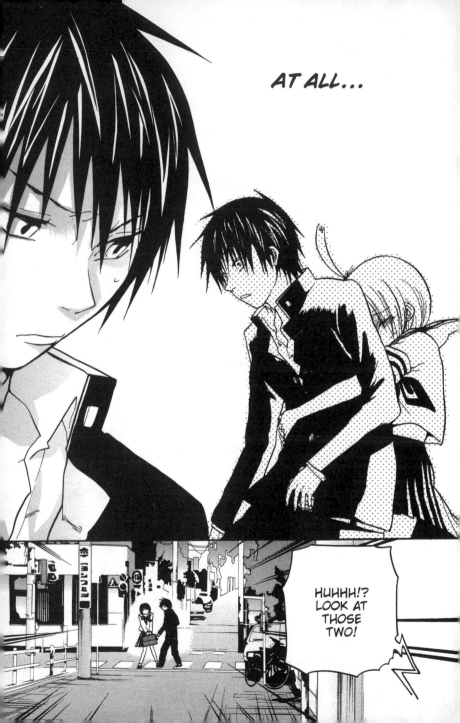

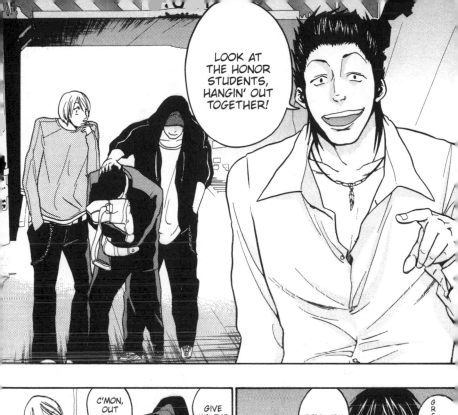

LOOK AT THE HONOR STUDENTS, HANGIN' OUT TOGETHER!

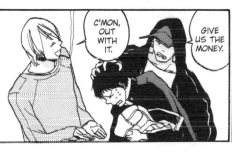

C'MON, OUT WITH IT.

GIVE US THE MONEY.

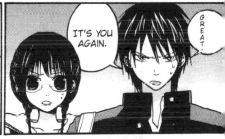

IT'S YOU AGAIN.

GREAT

NO!

WE CAN'T LET THEM GET AWAY WITH THIS!

CLASS REP!

H-HEY!

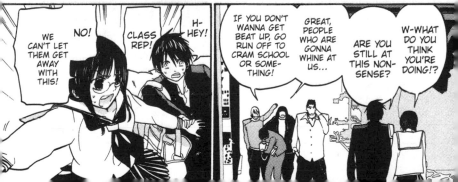

IF YOU DON'T WANNA GET BEAT UP, GO RUN OFF TO CRAM SCHOOL OR SOMETHING!

GREAT, PEOPLE WHO ARE GONNA WHINE AT US...

ARE YOU STILL AT THIS NONSENSE?

W-WHAT DO YOU THINK YOU'RE DOING!?

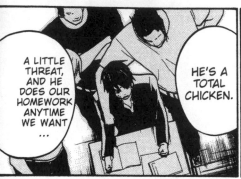

A LITTLE THREAT, AND HE DOES OUR HOMEWORK ANYTIME WE WANT...

HE'S A TOTAL CHICKEN.

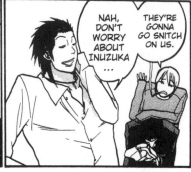

NAH, DON'T WORRY ABOUT INUZUKA...

THEY'RE GONNA GO SNITCH ON US.

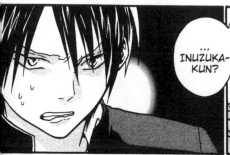

...INUZUKA-KUN?

RIGHT...

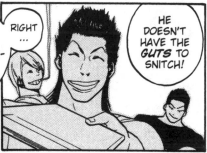

HE DOESN'T HAVE THE *GUTS* TO SNITCH!

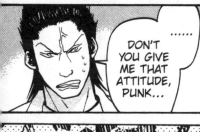

......

DON'T YOU GIVE ME THAT ATTITUDE, PUNK...

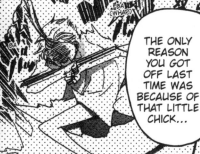

KBAM (WHAP)

THE ONLY REASON YOU GOT OFF LAST TIME WAS BECAUSE OF THAT LITTLE CHICK...

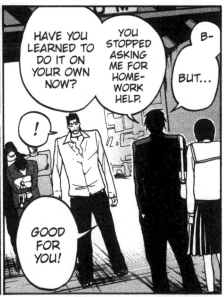

HAVE YOU LEARNED TO DO IT ON YOUR OWN NOW?

YOU STOPPED ASKING ME FOR HOMEWORK HELP.

B-BUT...

!

GOOD FOR YOU!

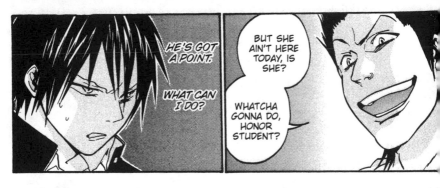

HE'S GOT A POINT.

WHAT CAN I DO?

BUT SHE AIN'T HERE TODAY, IS SHE?

WHATCHA GONNA DO, HONOR STUDENT?

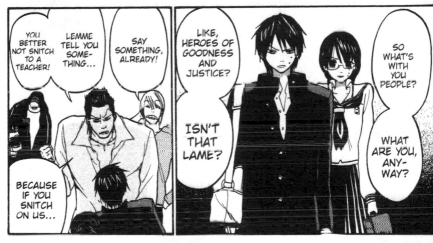

YOU BETTER NOT SNITCH TO A TEACHER!

LEMME TELL YOU SOMETHING...

SAY SOMETHING, ALREADY!

BECAUSE IF YOU SNITCH ON US...

LIKE, HEROES OF GOODNESS AND JUSTICE?

ISN'T THAT LAME?

SO WHAT'S WITH YOU PEOPLE?

WHAT ARE YOU, ANY-WAY?

SFX: GUWA (SWOOSH)

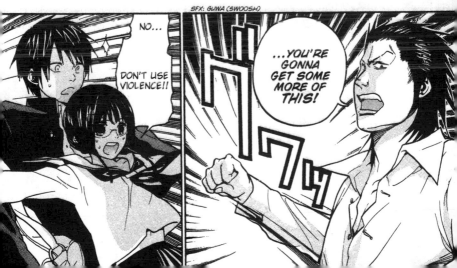

NO...

DON'T USE VIOLENCE!!

...YOU'RE GONNA GET SOME MORE OF THIS!

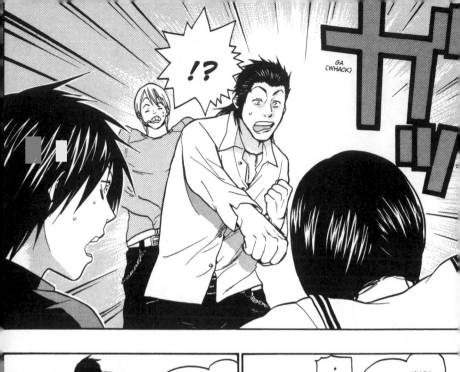

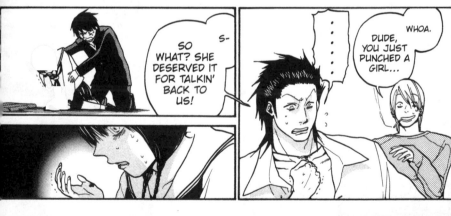

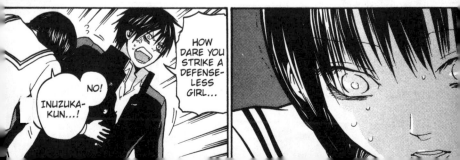

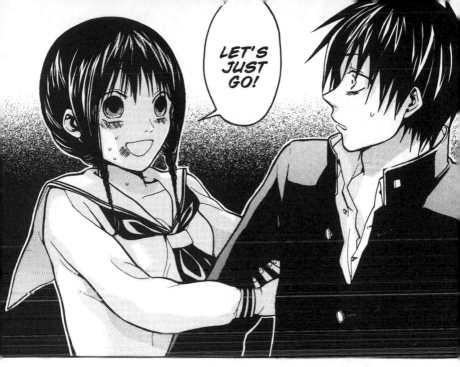

LET'S JUST GO!

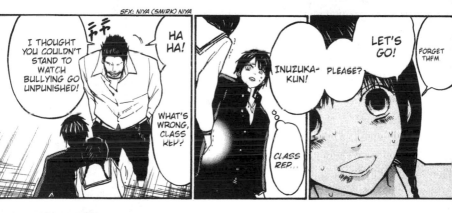

I THOUGHT YOU COULDN'T STAND TO WATCH BULLYING GO UNPUNISHED!

HA HA!

WHAT'S WRONG, CLASS REP?

INUZUKA-KUN!

PLEASE?

LET'S GO!

FORGET THEM

CLASS REP...

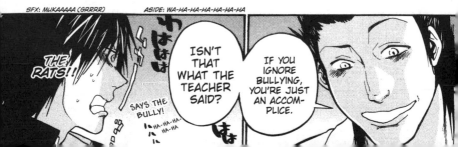

THE RATS!!

ISN'T THAT WHAT THE TEACHER SAID?

IF YOU IGNORE BULLYING, YOU'RE JUST AN ACCOMPLICE.

SAYS THE BULLY!

HA-HA-HA-HA-HA-HA

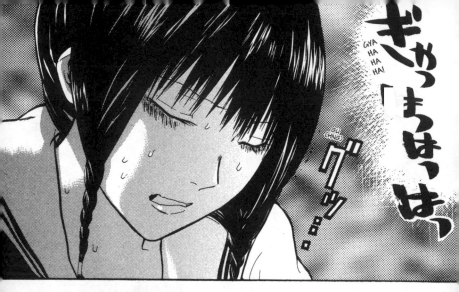

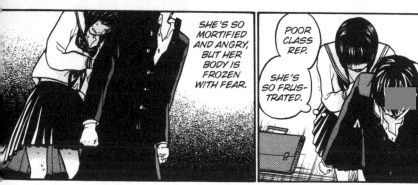

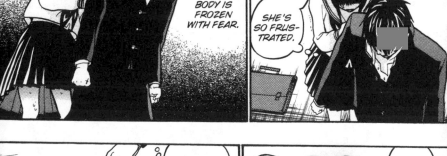

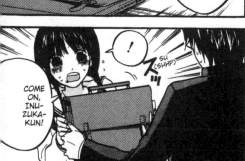

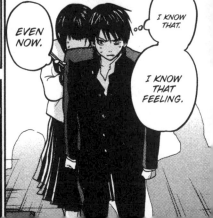

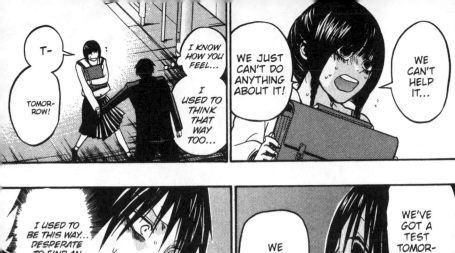

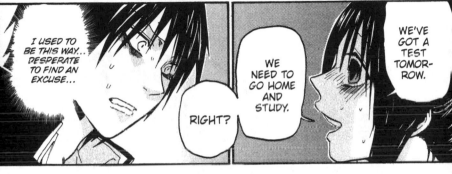

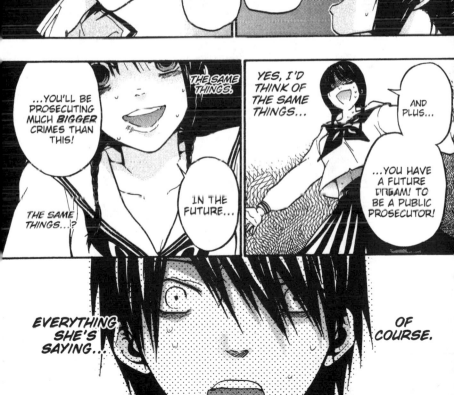

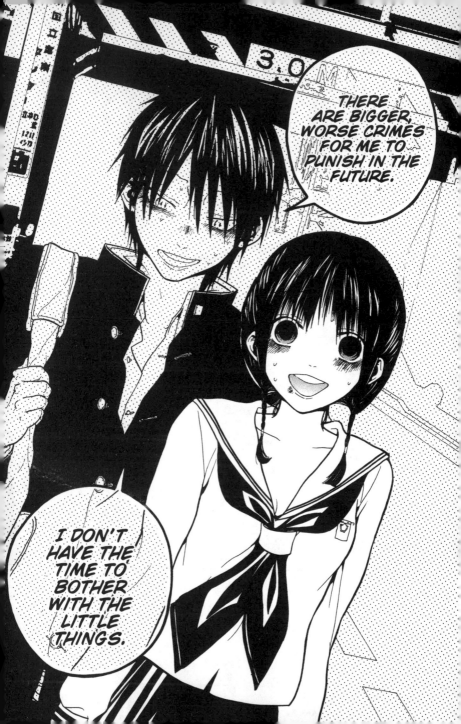

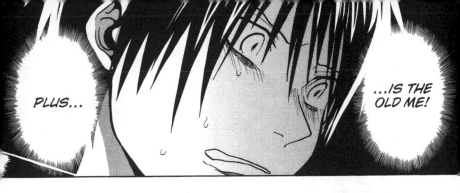

PLUS...

...IS THE OLD ME!

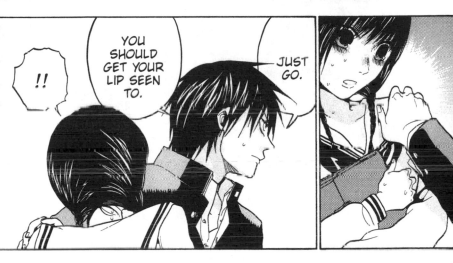

!!

YOU SHOULD GET YOUR LIP SEEN TO.

JUST GO.

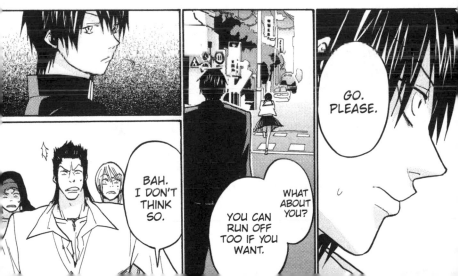

BAH. I DON'T THINK SO.

YOU CAN RUN OFF TOO IF YOU WANT.

WHAT ABOUT YOU?

GO. PLEASE.

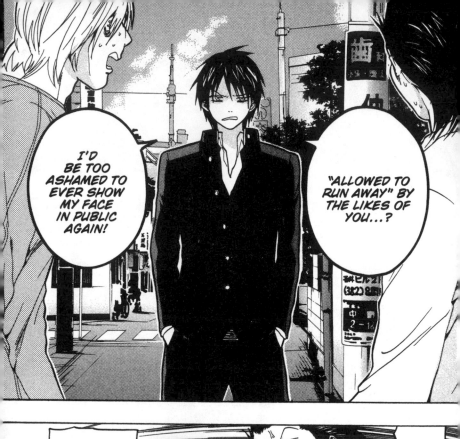

I'D BE TOO ASHAMED TO EVER SHOW MY FACE IN PUBLIC AGAIN!

"ALLOWED TO RUN AWAY" BY THE LIKES OF YOU...?

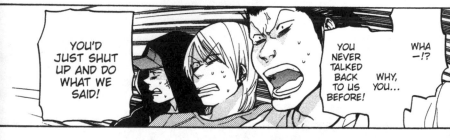

YOU'D JUST SHUT UP AND DO WHAT WE SAID!

YOU NEVER TALKED BACK TO US BEFORE!

WHY, YOU...

WHA—!?

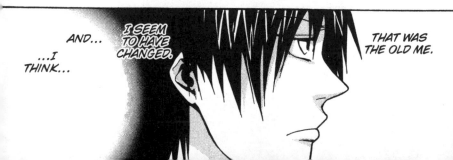

AND...

...I THINK...

I SEEM TO HAVE CHANGED.

THAT WAS THE OLD ME.

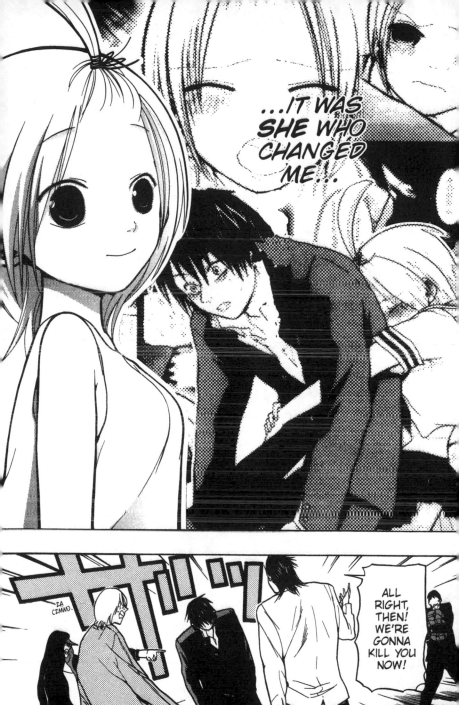

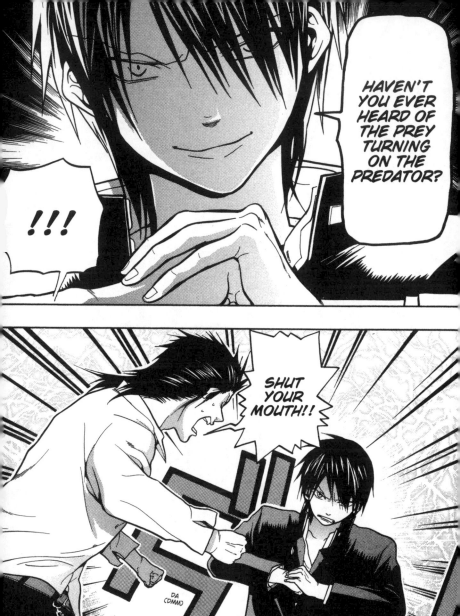

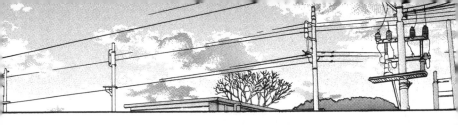

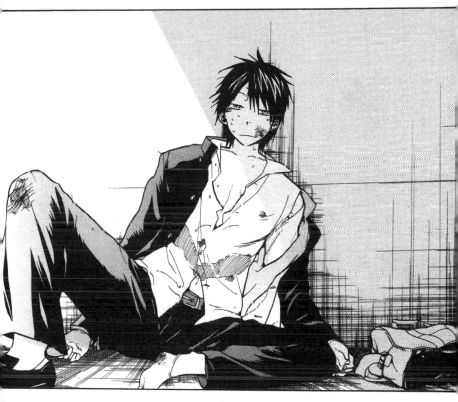

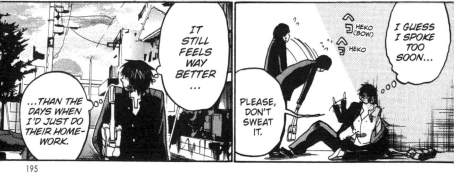

...THAN THE DAYS WHEN I'D JUST DO THEIR HOME-WORK.

IT STILL FEELS WAY BETTER...

PLEASE, DON'T SWEAT IT.

HEKO (BOW)

HEKO

I GUESS I SPOKE TOO SOON...

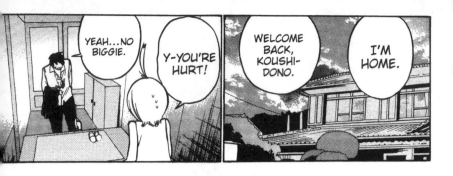

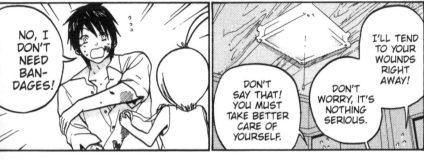

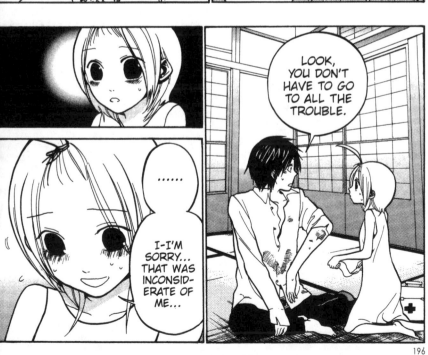

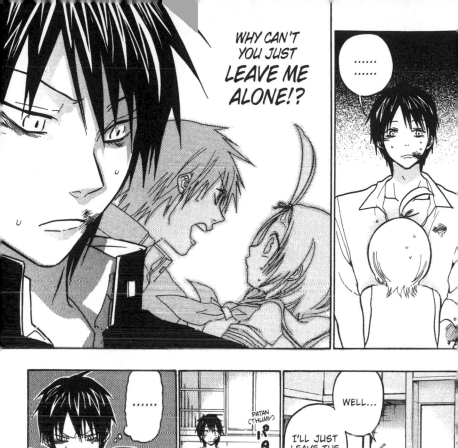

WHY CAN'T YOU JUST **LEAVE ME ALONE!?**

......
......

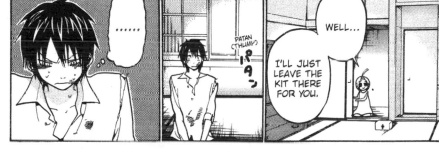

......

PATAN (THUMP)

WELL...

I'LL JUST LEAVE THE KIT THERE FOR YOU.

SFX: GARA (SHHK)

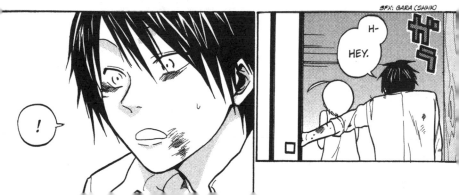

H- HEY.

!

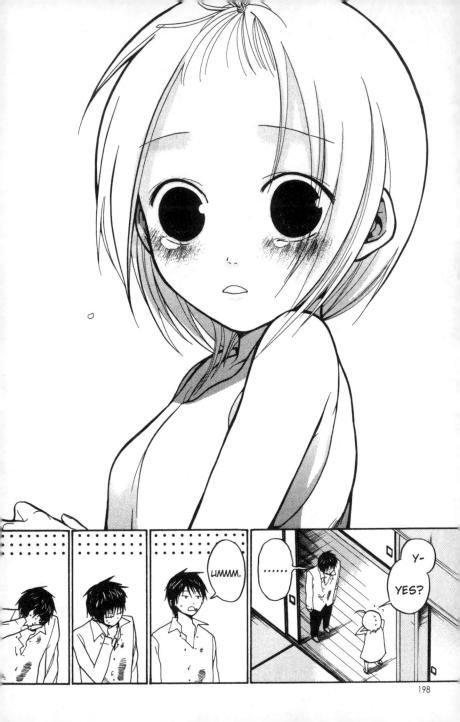

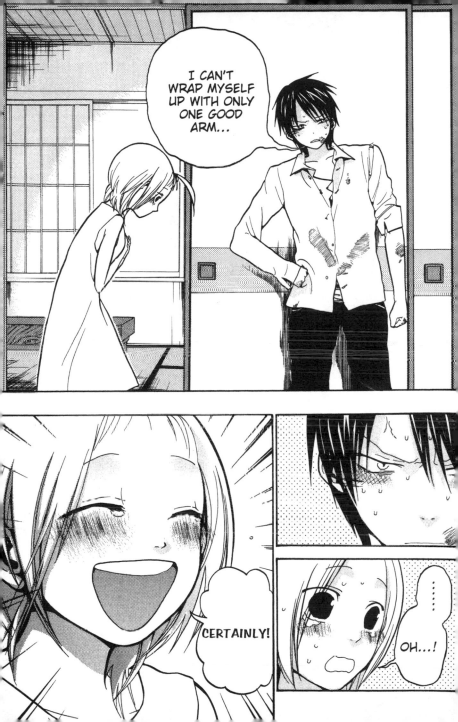

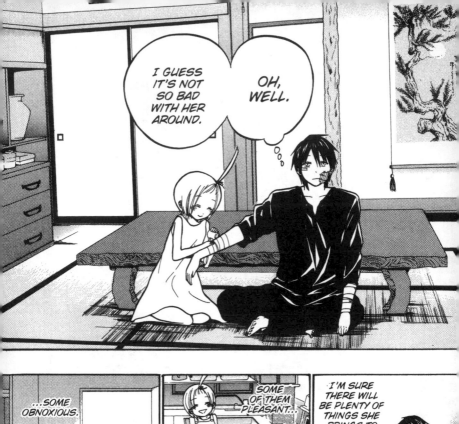

I GUESS IT'S NOT SO BAD WITH HER AROUND.

OH, WELL.

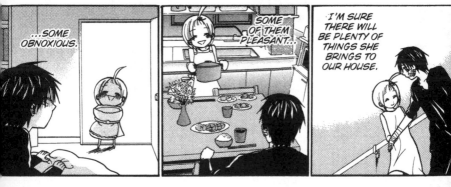

...SOME OBNOXIOUS.

SOME OF THEM PLEASANT...

I'M SURE THERE WILL BE PLENTY OF THINGS SHE BRINGS TO OUR HOUSE.

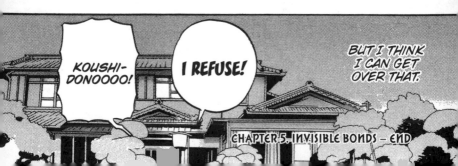

KOUSHI-DONOOOO!

I REFUSE!

BUT I THINK I CAN GET OVER THAT.

CHAPTER 5. INVISIBLE BONDS – END

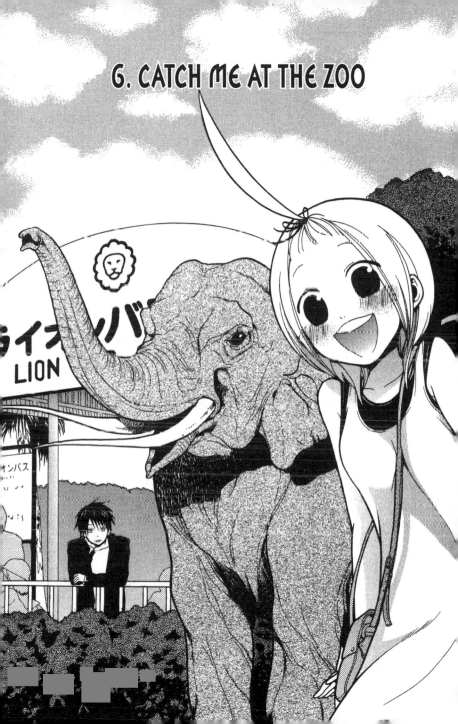

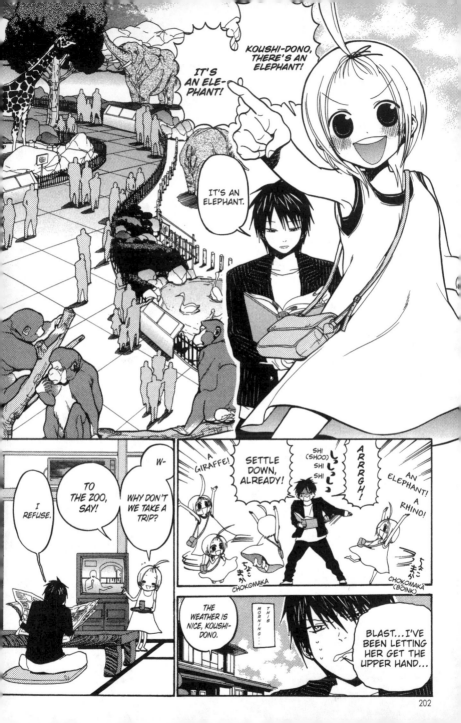

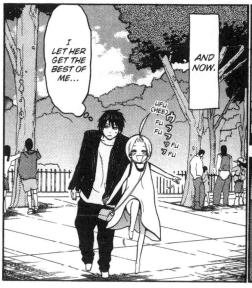

I LET HER GET THE BEST OF ME...

AND NOW.

UFU (HEE) FU FU FU FU FU

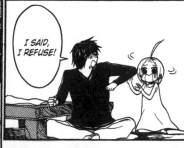

I SAID, I REFUSE!

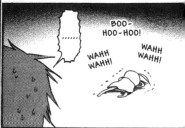

......

BOO-HOO-HOO!

WAHH WAHH!

WAHH WAHH!

SFX: HYOKKO (PRANCE)

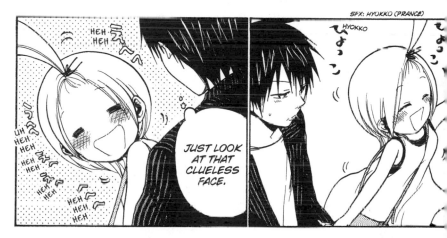

HEH HEH

HYOKKO

UH HEH HEH HEH HEH HEH HEH HEH HEH HEH HEH HEH

JUST LOOK AT THAT CLUELESS FACE.

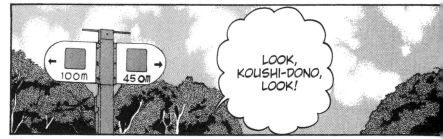

100M

450M

LOOK, KOUSHI-DONO, LOOK!

203

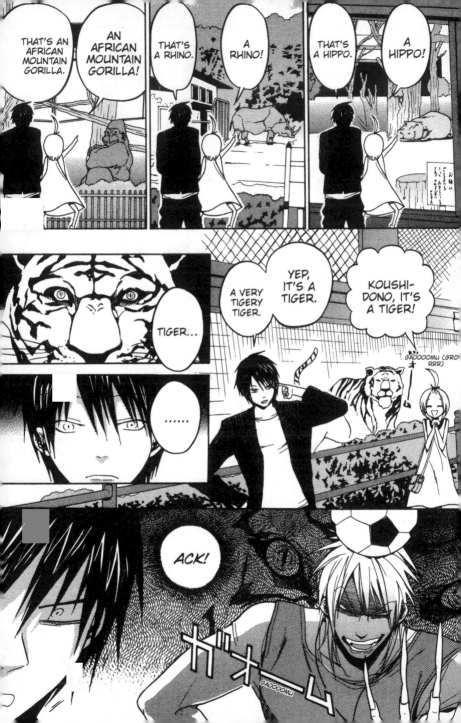

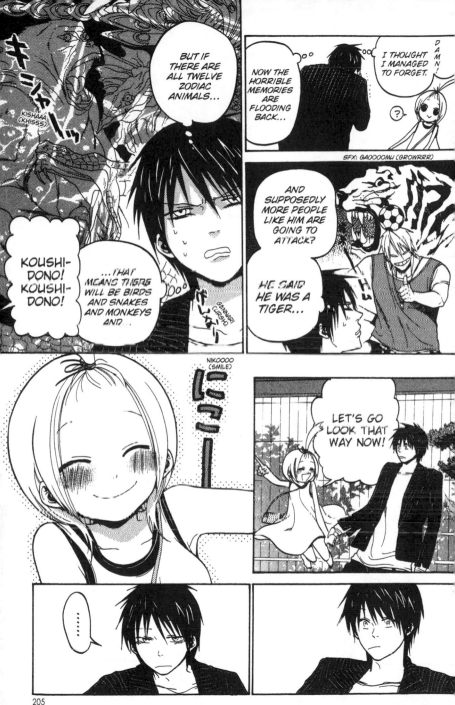

KISHAAA
(KHISSS)

BUT IF THERE ARE ALL TWELVE ZODIAC ANIMALS...

NOW THE HORRIBLE MEMORIES ARE FLOODING BACK...

I THOUGHT I MANAGED TO FORGET.

DAMN!

SFX: GAOOOOMU (GROWRRR)

AND SUPPOSEDLY MORE PEOPLE LIKE HIM ARE GOING TO ATTACK?

HE SAID HE WAS A TIGER...

KOUSHI-DONO! KOUSHI-DONO!

...THAT MEANS TIGERS WILL BE BIRDS AND SNAKES AND MONKEYS AND...

NIKOOOO (SMILE)

LET'S GO LOOK THAT WAY NOW!

......

205

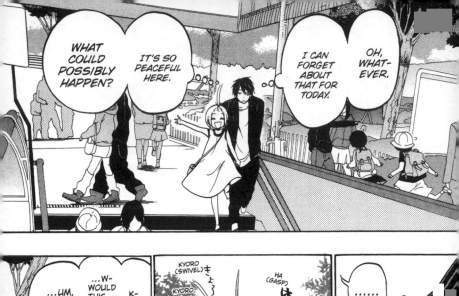

WHAT COULD POSSIBLY HAPPEN?

IT'S SO PEACEFUL HERE.

I CAN FORGET ABOUT THAT FOR TODAY.

OH, WHAT-EVER.

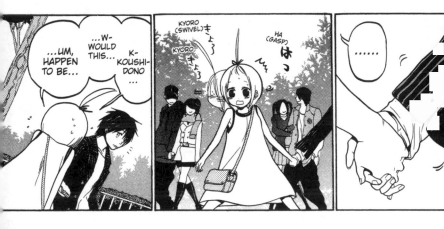

...UM, WOULD THIS...

...W-WOULD THIS... K-KOUSHI-DONO...

KYORO (SWIVEL)

KYORO

HA (GASP)

......

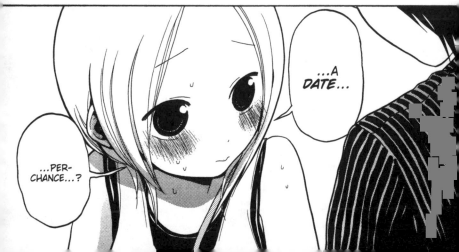

...A DATE...

...PER-CHANCE...?

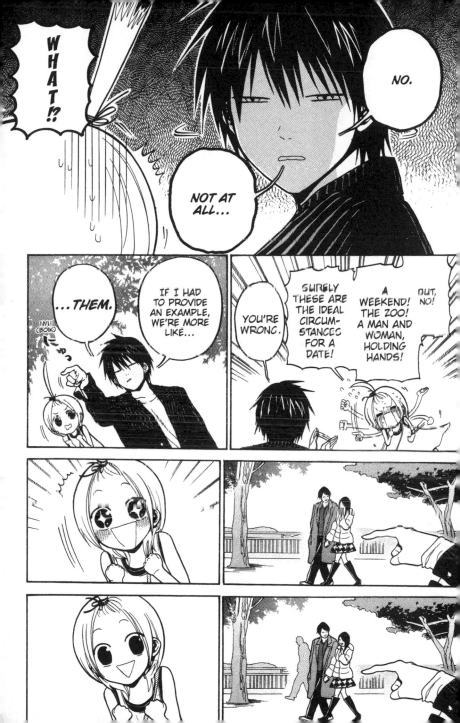

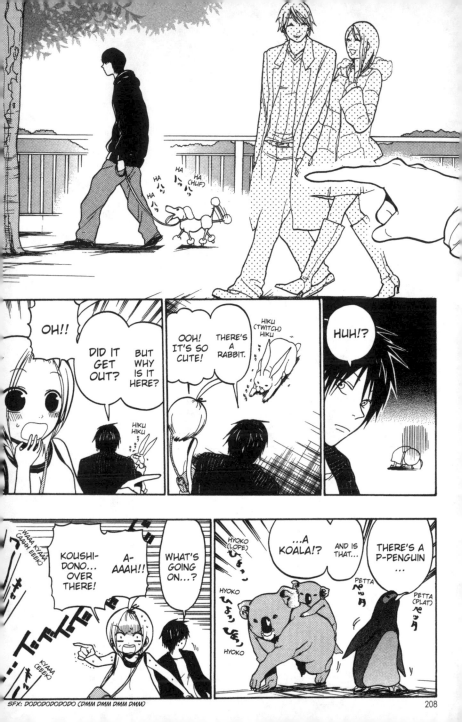

HA♪ HA♪ HA (HUF)
HA♪

OH!!

DID IT GET OUT?

BUT WHY IS IT HERE?

HIKU HIKU

OOH! IT'S SO CUTE!

THERE'S A RABBIT.

HIKU (TWITCH) HIKU

HUH!?

WAAA KYAAA (AAH! EEEK)

KOUSHI-DONO... OVER THERE!

A-AAAH!!

WHAT'S GOING ON...?

KYAAA (EEEK)

HYOKO (LOPE)

...A KOALA!?

AND IS THAT...

THERE'S A P-PENGUIN...

PETTA (PLAT)

HYOKO

PETTA (PLAT)

HYOKO

SFX: DODODODODODO (DMM DMM DMM DMM)

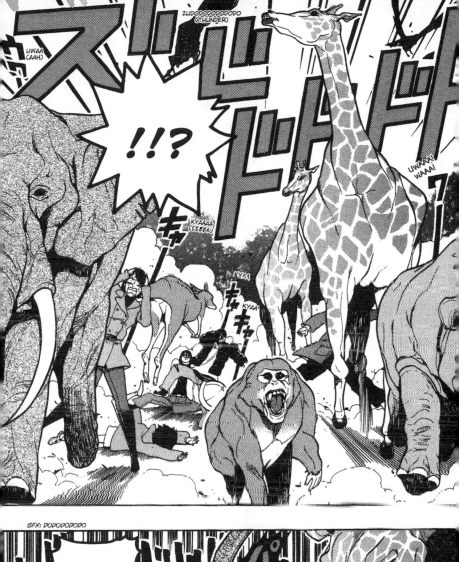

UWAA (AAH)

ZUDODODODODO (STHUNDER)

!!?

KYA

KYAAAA (EEEEK)

KYA

KYAA

UWAAA! WAAA!

SFX: DODODODODO

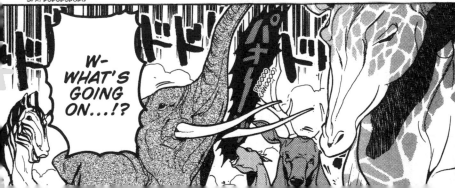

W-WHAT'S GOING ON...!?

PAOOO (AAOOO)

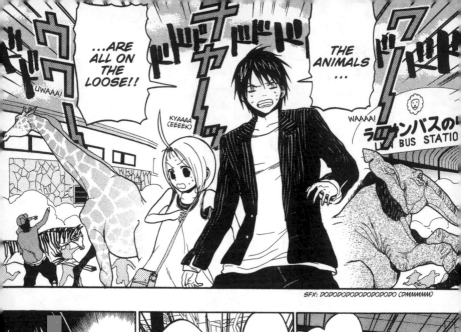

THE ANIMALS ...

...ARE ALL ON THE LOOSE!!

BUS STATIO

SFX: DODODODODODODODODO (DMMMMM)

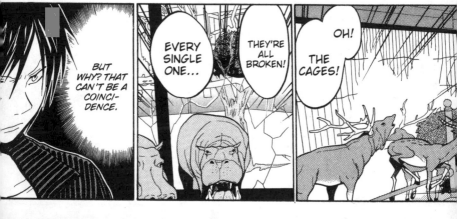

BUT WHY? THAT CAN'T BE A COINCIDENCE.

EVERY SINGLE ONE...

THEY'RE ALL BROKEN!

OH! THE CAGES!

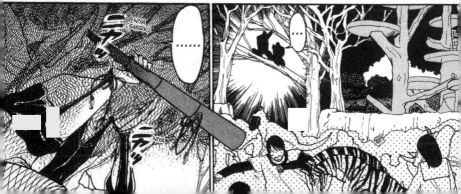

......

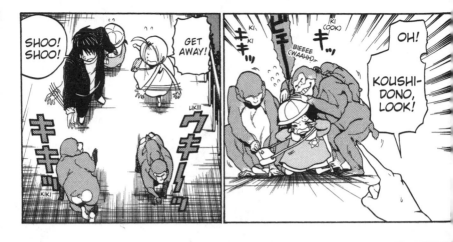

SHOO! SHOO!

GET AWAY!

KI, KI, KI

KI (COOK)

BIEEEE (WAAHD...)

KI...

OH!

KOUSHI-DONO, LOOK!

UKI!!!

KIKI

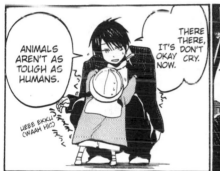

ANIMALS AREN'T AS TOUGH AS HUMANS.

THERE THERE, IT'S OKAY NOW. DON'T CRY.

UEEE EKKU (WAAH HIC)

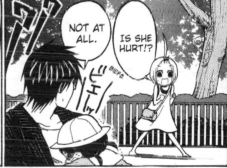

NOT AT ALL.

IS SHE HURT!?

BIEFE

SFX: HIKKU (CHIC) HIKKU   SFX: WAAH WAAH

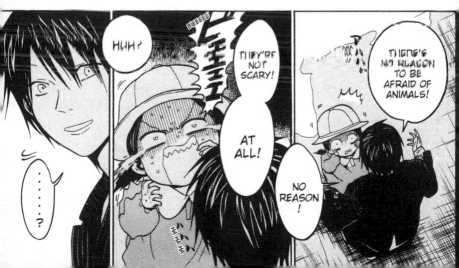

HUH?

BIEEEED

THEY'RE NOT SCARY!

AT ALL!

NO REASON!

THERE'S NO REASON TO BE AFRAID OF ANIMALS!

· · · · · ?

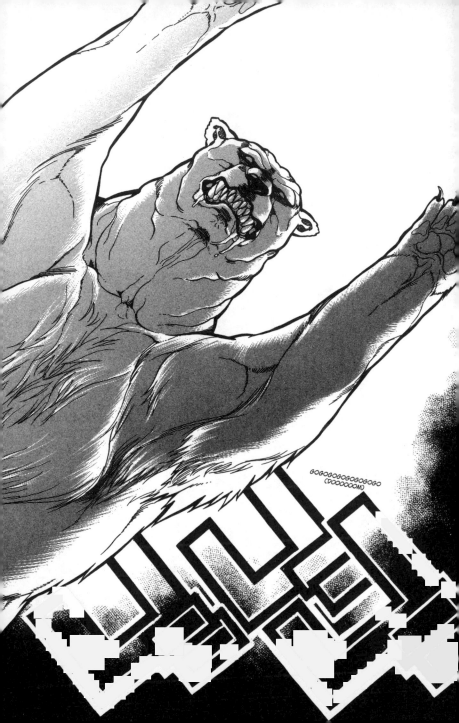

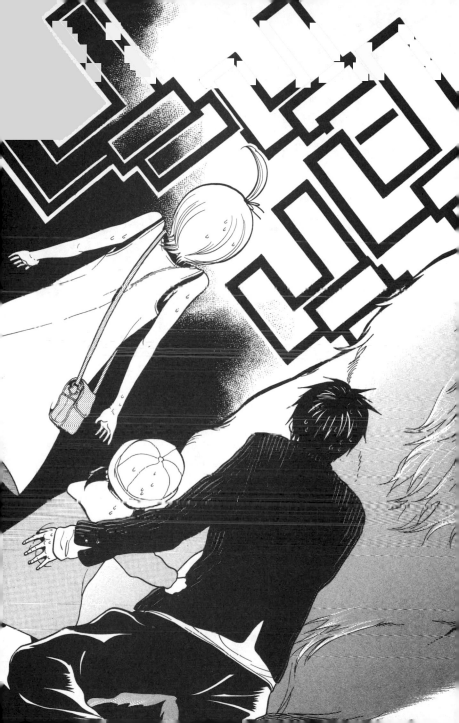

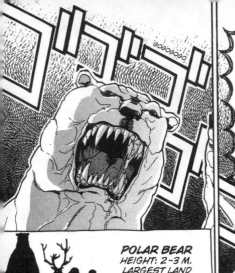

GOGOGOGO

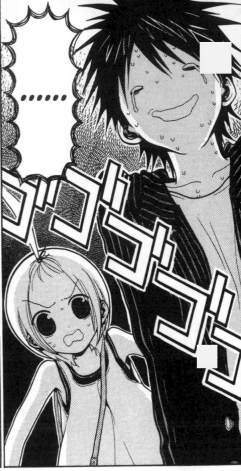

......

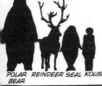

POLAR BEAR
HEIGHT: 2~3 M.
LARGEST LAND
CARNIVORE.
MAIN PREY: SEAL.
LOVES REINDEER
TOO.

POLAR REINDEER SEAL KOUSHI
BEAR

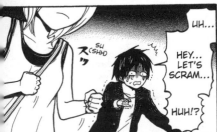

SU
(SHH)

UH...

HEY...
LET'S
SCRAM...

HUH!?

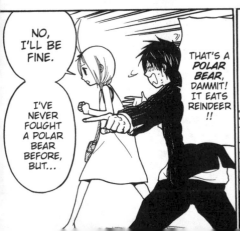

NO,
I'LL BE
FINE.

I'VE
NEVER
FOUGHT
A POLAR
BEAR
BEFORE,
BUT...

THAT'S A
**POLAR
BEAR,**
DAMMIT!
IT EATS
REINDEER
!!

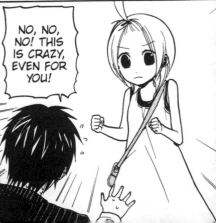

NO, NO,
NO! THIS
IS CRAZY,
EVEN FOR
YOU!

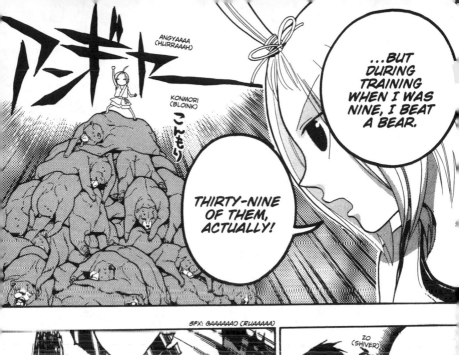

ANGYAAAA (URRRAAAH)

KONMORI (BLOINK)
こんもり

...BUT DURING TRAINING WHEN I WAS NINE, I BEAT A BEAR.

THIRTY-NINE OF THEM, ACTUALLY!

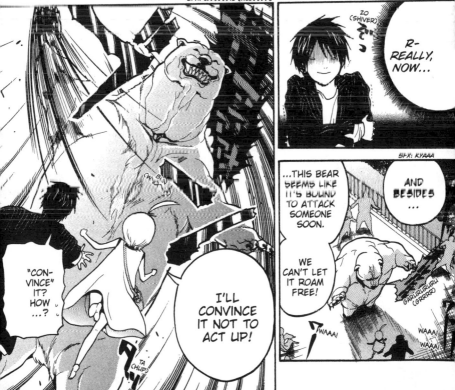

SFX: GAAAAAAO (RUAAAAA)

ZO (SHIVER)

R-REALLY, NOW...

SFX: KYAAA

...THIS BEAR SEEMS LIKE IT'S BOUND TO ATTACK SOMEONE SOON.

AND BESIDES...

WE CAN'T LET IT ROAM FREE!

"CONVINCE" IT? HOW...?

I'LL CONVINCE IT NOT TO ACT UP!

GARURURURU (GRRRRR)

WAAA!

WAAA! WAAA!

TA (CHUP)

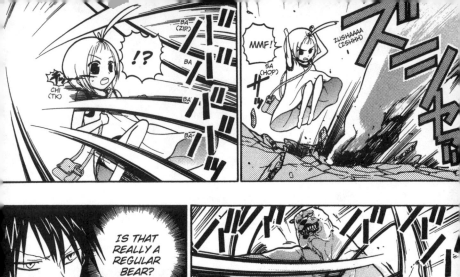

SFX: BABA BABABA BABABA

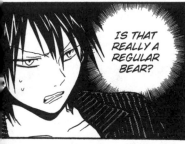

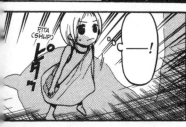

SFX: GIRAA (GRING)

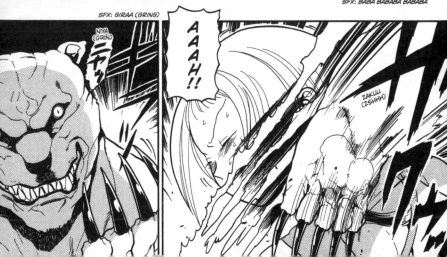

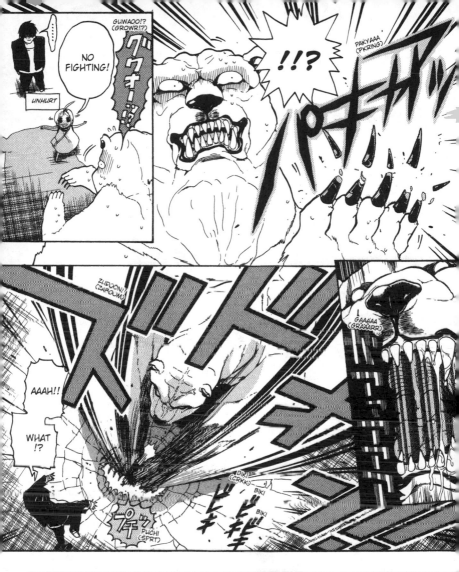

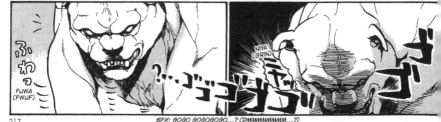

SFX: GOGO GOGOGOGO...? (DMMMMMMMM...?)

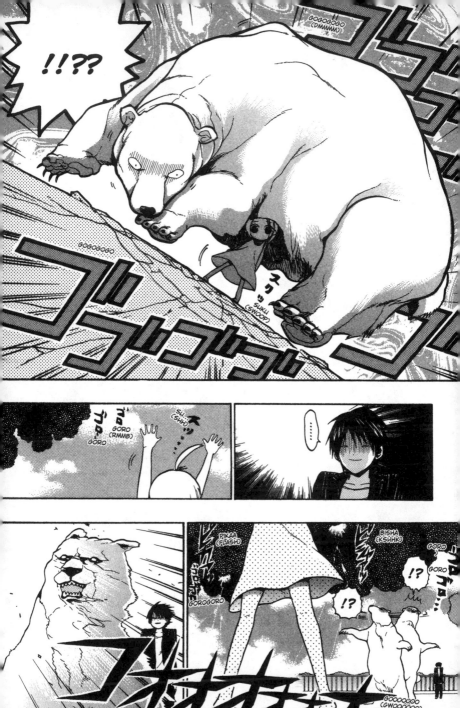

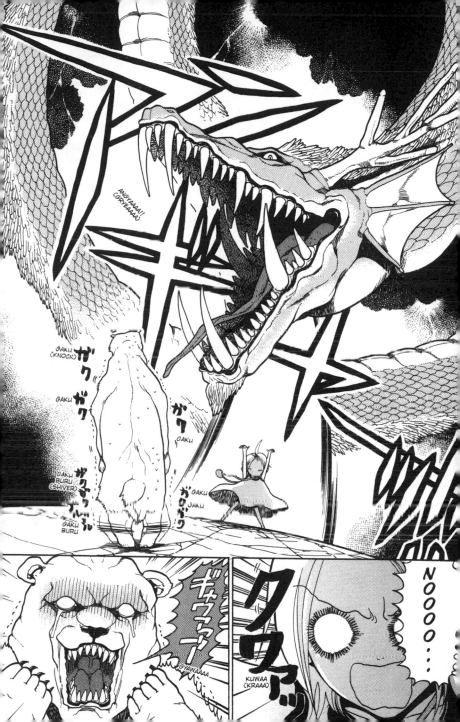

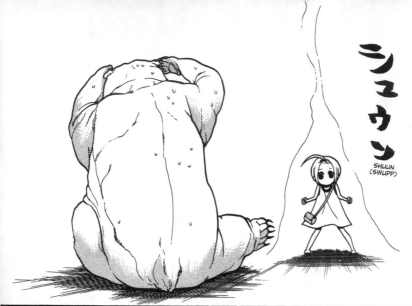

シュゥン
SHUUN
(SWUPP)

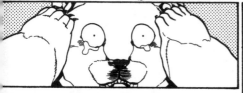

...FIGHTING...

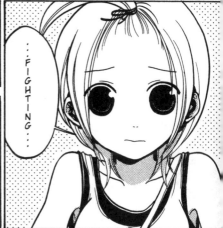

I THINK IT'S LEARNED ITS LESSON...

KOSO (WHSS)

H-HEY! DO YOUR USUAL THING!

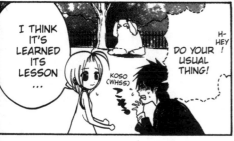

YIKES...

Y-

YOU'RE REALLY SOME-THING...

EEK! HEE! HEE!

GORO

GORO (LICK)

BURURU (BRR)

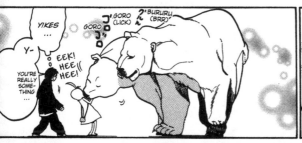

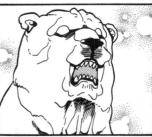

220

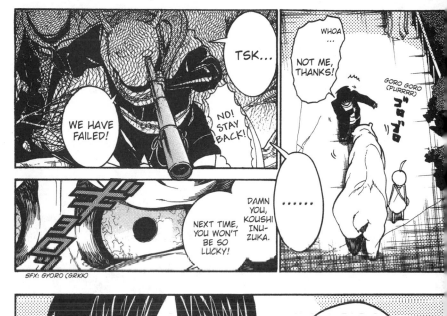

TSK...

WE HAVE FAILED!

NO! STAY BACK!

NEXT TIME, YOU WON'T BE SO LUCKY!

......

DAMN YOU, KOUSHI INU-ZUKA.

WHOA...

NOT ME, THANKS!

GORO GORO (PURRRR)

SFX: GYORO (GRKK)

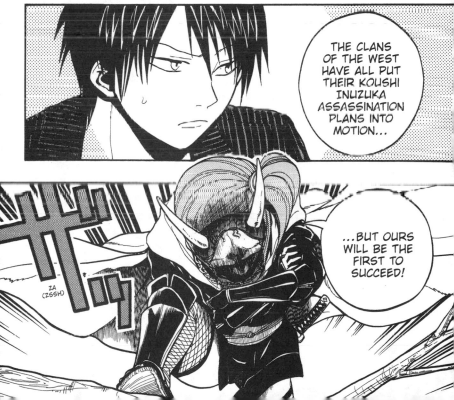

THE CLANS OF THE WEST HAVE ALL PUT THEIR KOUSHI INUIZUKA ASSASSINATION PLANS INTO MOTION...

...BUT OURS WILL BE THE FIRST TO SUCCEED!

ZA (ZSSH)

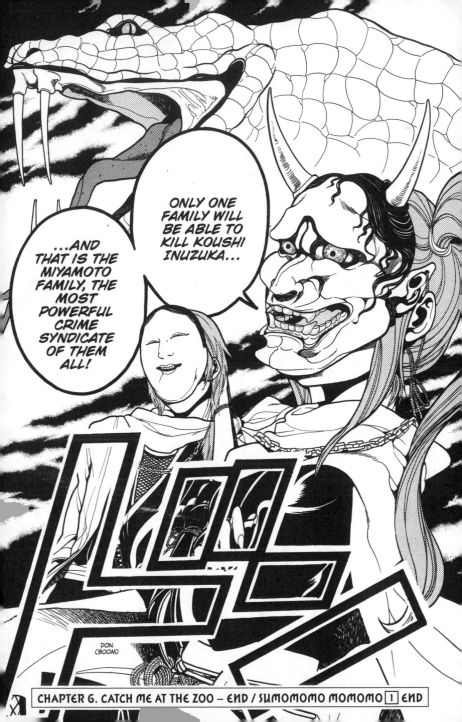

TRANSLATION NOTES

Sumomomo Momomo is part of a well-known Japanese tongue twister which reads, "*Sumomo mo momo mo momo no uchi,*" and roughly means,"Plums and peaches are part of the peach family."

Page 3
Haira Ichiden Musou-ryuu Secret Art: Sounds like a mouthful, doesn't it? This translates roughly to "Haira Line Peerless-Style Secret Art." Haira is the name of one of twelve heavenly generals that are said to protect Yakushi Nyorai, the Buddha of Medicine. They are each associated with one of the twelve Chinese zodiac animals. In the particular grouping which concerns this story, Haira is connected to the "dragon"...which just happens to be one of the symbols in Momoko's family name, Kuzuryuu.

Page 7
Basara Fudou Shingan ryuu: This means, roughly, "Basara Immovable Mind's-Eye-Style." Like Haira, Basara is another of the twelve heavenly generals, but he corresponds to the "dog" sign of the Chinese zodiac. Just like in Momoko's case, the character for "dog" is in Koushi's family name (Inuzuka).

Page 12
Osu: A common greeting in martial arts.

-dono: An honorific suffix. While originally meaning "lord," dono came to be used for people of rank to show respect. It is used rarely in modern times. Momoko's frequent use of "dono" in the series is part of her archaic and formal speech.

Page 13
Six Codes: The six main legal codes (or areas of law) that make up the main body of Japanese law. They are: the Civil Code, Commercial Code, Criminal Code, Constitution of Japan, Code of Criminal Procedure, and Code of Civil Procedure.

Page 94
The Twelve Martial Arts Families each correspond to the twelve animals of the Chinese zodiac, which include the dog (*inu* in Inuzuka) and the dragon (*ryuu* in Kuzuryuu).

Page 101
Shindara Rettetsu-ryuu: This translates to "Shindara Fierce Iron Style." Shindara is another of the heavenly generals, associated with the tiger of the Chinese Zodiac. As with Koushi and Momoko, the character for "tiger" appears in the name "Koganei."

Page 123
Hara-Kiri is the colloquial term for the ritualistic form of suicide known as *seppuku* (See below). The literal translation is "cutting the belly."

Page 147
Plastic bottles: There is a very common urban legend in Japan that says cats are wary of plastic bottles filled with water and will avoid them. Studies have shown that this is completely untrue, but nevertheless it is a well-circulated piece of modern folklore.

Page 150
Seppuku is a ritualistic form of suicide practiced by Japan's samurai. Generally it is characterized by self-disembowelment using a sword stroke from the left to the right of the belly and was often regarded as a means of retaining one's honor.

Page 155
Mortal enemies/Marriage: As you can tell, there is a pun at work here, which we were able to work into English fairly close to the original. In Japanese, the confusion is between the words "*kekkon*" (marriage) and "*ketto*" (duel), which both share the letters "*ke*" at the start.

Page 159
Jinshin War: A succession dispute that broke out following the death of Emperor Tenji in 672 A.D.

Genpei Wars: A series of conflicts between the Taira and Minamoto clans from 1180-1185. Led to the establishment of the Kamakura shogunate.

Nanboku-cho Wars: A long period of wars between the Northern and Southern Imperial Courts of Japan, from 1336-1392.

Onin War: A civil war from 1467-1477 that initiated the "Warring States" period (*Sengoku-jidai*) during which many daimyo fought to control all of Japan.

Battles of Kawanakajima: A series of battles between the Takeda and Uesugi clans on the plain of Kawanakajima from 1553-1564, during the Warring States period.

Boshin War: A civil war fought in 1868-1869 between the military Tokugawa shogunate and the supporters of the imperial court.

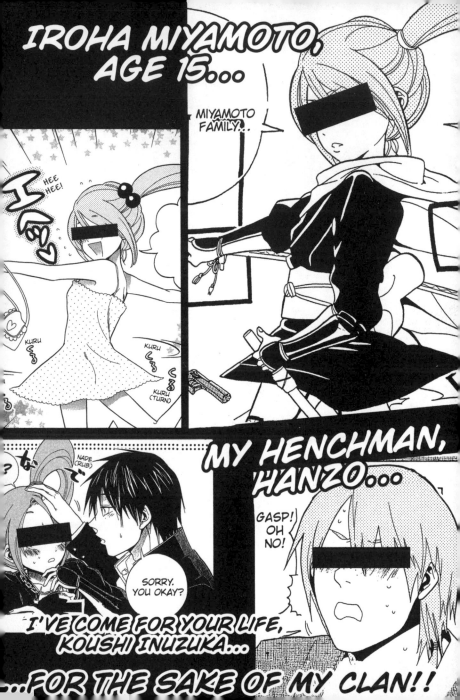

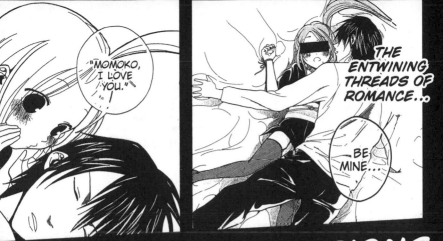

"MOMOKO, I LOVE YOU."

THE ENTWINING THREADS OF ROMANCE...

BE MINE...

THE FIERCE COLLISIONS OF HUMAN DRAMA.

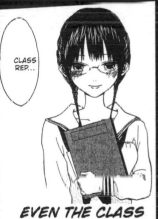

CLASS REP...

EVEN THE CLASS REPRESENTATIVE...

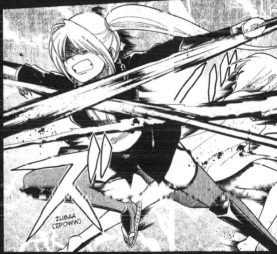

ZUBAA (ZPOWW)

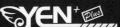

SUMOMOMO MOMOMO ①

SHINOBU OHTAKA

Translation: Stephen Paul

Lettering: Terri Delgado

SUMOMOMO MOMOMO Vol. 1 © 2005 Shinobu Ohtaka / SQUARE ENIX.
All rights reserved. First published in Japan in 2005 by SQUARE ENIX
CO., LTD. English translation rights arranged with SQUARE ENIX CO.,
LTD. and Hachette Book Group through Tuttle-Mori Agency, Inc.

Translation © 2009 by SQUARE ENIX CO., LTD.

Yen Press
Hachette Book Group
237 Park Avenue, New York, NY 10017

Visit our Web sites at www.HachetteBookGroup.com and
www.YenPress.com.

Yen Press is an imprint of Hachette Book Group, Inc. The Yen Press
name and logo are trademarks of Hachette Book Group, Inc.

First Yen Press Edition: May 2009

ISBN: 978-0-7595-3004-1

10 9 8 7 6 5 4 3 2 1

BVG

Printed in the United States of America